BETWEEN
MOUNTAIN AND MARSH

PLÂS MACHEN   M. EDMONDS.

[see page 127

Between Mountain and Marsh

in the
Hundred of Wentllwg
Monmouthshire

BY

J. ANTONY F. PICKFORD

B.A. OXON.

President Oxford Union Society, 1944

WITH
FOREWORD BY SIR CYRIL FOX, P.S.A., F.B.A.
Director National Museum of Wales

AND ILLUSTRATED BY MICHAEL EDMONDS

R. H. JOHNS LIMITED
Publishers
NEWPORT
MON.

FIRST PUBLISHED DEC. 1946

Printed in Great Britain
at the Press of
R. H. Johns Limited
Newport : Mon.

ACKNOWLEDGEMENTS

TOO many people have talked to me, encouraged, suggested and helped, for me to mention all by name, but in Bassaleg itself the names of the Vicar, the Rev. A. G. A. Picton, of Mr. Vaughan of Pentrepoeth, and of Mr. David Powell of Rhiwderin spring immediately to mind. Others have lent me books or let me ramble inquisitively over their houses and to all of them I am deeply indebted. Outside Bassaleg my thanks are due to Sir Cyril Fox, Director of the National Museum of Wales, for help such as only he could give with Croes-heolydd farm and for advice on the whole prehistoric period; to Professor Ifor Williams of Bangor, for a most illuminating letter and an article, both on Bassaleg as a place-name; also to Messrs. Davis, Lloyds and Wilson, who let me see the records of the Manor of Bassaleg. Finally I must acknowledge the unfailing kindness and co-operation of the Rev. Thomas Williams, the Rev. F. A. Oswell, the Rev. Hopkin Evans, Rectors respectively of Bedwas, Machen and Llanvihangel Fedw, and also of Mr. John Warner, Newport Borough Librarian, who started fresh hares whenever the course looked empty.

A.P.

The untimely death of the author occurred on 31st May, 1946, when the final proofs were awaiting his revision.

The Publishers wish to express their grateful thanks to Sir Cyril Fox, P.S.A., F.B.A., *Director of the National*

Museum of Wales, for kindly writing the Foreword and so fulfilling an expressed personal desire of the Author and also to Mr. John Warner, F.L.A., Newport Borough Librarian and Mr. J. R. Gabriel, M.A., Hon. Sec., Monmouthshire and Caerleon Antiquarian Association, for so very willingly undertaking the difficult task of checking the final proofs in as many particulars as the circumstances permitted.

This co-operation did much to make possible the publication of the volume, which is truly a memorial to the gifted and promising author.

CONTENTS

10 CONTENTS

LIST OF ILLUSTRATIONS

SPECIALLY DRAWN BY MICHAEL EDMONDS

FOREWORD

The Publishers of " Between Mountain and Marsh " have sent to me the final proof of the book, informing me of the author's death, and requesting me to write a " Foreword " to it. This request has been reinforced by the expressed wish of Antony Pickford's family, and by the intimation that he had intended himself to ask me to do this.

Antony Pickford was born at Newport, Monmouthshire, on October 30th, 1922. He was educated at Bryanston, and at Oriel College, Oxford, where in 1944 he took his degree in Law, with second class honours. He was also successively Librarian, Secretary and President of the Oxford Union Society. To those people who knew how he had to battle against ill-health his unfailing cheerfulness and energy, physical and mental, were a great source of wonder. He died in May, 1946.

My acquaintance with Antony began before the war, when he sought at the Museum information about the antiquities of the Bassaleg district. Thereafter I accompanied him on two or three occasions to hillfort, church and farm; the range of his interests, archæological, antiquarian and historical, the seriousness of his purpose in life, and the quickness of his apprehension, seemed to me unusual in a young man. He presented, I judge, promise of a high usefulness to county and State, and his untimely death means more than a severe personal loss to his family.

It will be clear to the reader that the book lacks that revision which, had he lived, the author would have given it. This is a pity; but what the book would have gained in the apparatus of scholarship, and the increased accuracy which would have resulted from the laborious verifying of references which is part of an author's duty, might have resulted in such changes in the text as would have destroyed its chief charm—vividness and spontaneity. No one can read " Between Mountain and Marsh " who knows anything of the topography and character of the region with which it deals, without being inspired by a desire to follow Mr. Pickford in his tramps round the country, and to share his experiences, and his pleasure in discovery. That is the great value of the book—to reveal to a people disillusioned by world events, the simple and permanent delight which the environment of each and every one of us can give, if it be sought, in this lovely land of Wales.

CYRIL FOX,
National Museum of Wales.

14th September, 1946.

INTRODUCTION

THIS is a book of that part of the Hundred of Wentllwg (Wentlooge or Wentllwch) that lies between the Mountains and the Marsh. It will fill, I hope, a genuine need, for we in Wentllwg are by far the worst sufferers from that strange dearth of historians which afflicts what is, after all, one of Britain's most historic areas. Although we share Coxe with the rest of the County we were, alas, deprived of the services of Sir Joseph Bradney, who, after completing the history of the Hundreds of Abergavenny, Skenfrith, Raglan, Usk and Caldicot, died before coming over into Wentllwg. This very humble effort is intended as a temporary stop-gap for at least a part of that area.

The portion of Wentllwg with which I am going to deal was, in ancient times, by far the most habitable and therefore the most historic, and the chief difficulty before me, when I came to set out in readable form the mass of evidence that I had collected, was to know how best I could describe simply the whole district all through the vast length of time that has elapsed since Neolithic man first settled in Wales. I have adopted what I think is the best method. I have taken the key parish of Wentllwg, the ecclesiastical mother Parish, the Parish that is historically the most interesting from prehistoric times onward, the old Parish of Bassaleg. Around it I have tried, in succeeding chapters, to build up a picture of Wentllwg through the ages. Then, having completed my general picture through the medium of Bassaleg, I have attempted to fit in the historical facts about the other parishes so that readers may apply them to the structure of what has gone before and gain thereby an impression of the whole.

There is no doubt that Bassaleg has, for a Parish of its size, a long history. It is a social history for it cannot be found in any book; it is not a tale of Kings or of Princes, of Treaties or of Battles, rather it is a story of people—ordinary people, who lived and died leaving no lasting memorial save the ruins of the places in which they lived. Just once there came a man whose name will never be forgotten until Welsh poetry ceases to be sung but, apart from Dafydd ap Gwilym, Bassaleg does not aspire to greatness. All parishes have some history attached to them—it is implicit in the grey stone of their churches, but Bassaleg has a longer history than most. It is not only longer; it is more interesting and it covers a wider range.

Collecting material for such a work has not been easy, for nothing similar has previously been attempted. I took as a starting point the scanty observations of old Archdeacon Coxe and, when I put these together with the Ordnance Survey Map and local tradition, I soon found myself following endless threads of investigation and a multitude of fascinating clues. All too often they came to nothing, but sometimes a chance reference would reveal a new source, one thing would lead to another, and off one would go gathering information into the most unexpected places till at last a new piece of the puzzle was sorted out and ready to be fitted to the whole. It has meant long afternoons in the Bodleian Library and in the Libraries of Cardiff and Newport, it has meant long expeditions without petrol, and it has meant some excavation though, alas, all too little of that has been possible. It has been a fascinating task although as a spare time activity it has been a lengthy one. If, however, I have unravelled the twisted skein of the history of a piece of our countryside into a single thread of a story of human activity, I shall not have laboured in vain.

I would say here that I have not attempted to deal with the pedigrees of the great family of Morgan. That task was accomplished by Sir Joseph Bradney and it would be an impertinence on my part to repeat his work. It is accessible to all elsewhere.

But here and there, to illustrate the story of some person, place or building, it has been necessary to delve deeply into various family trees. Some discussion of pedigree is unavoidable when writing history—and mediæval Welsh history in particular—but I have done my best not to be over elaborate.

I am fully conscious that the book is full of imperfections—there are, doubtless, sources I have overlooked, wrong inferences I have drawn, rash generalities that I have made. Other mistakes are due to lack of scientific excavation or inaccessability of records. If, however, I waited till we knew everything about Wentllwg I should wait till the end of time. Here is but the extent of our knowledge at the present day and whatever may come to light in later years can be added hereto. In the meantime I should be very grateful for any point of information which I may have overlooked or fact which I have got completely wrong. These may be many and if so the responsibility is mine and I can only plead that I may not be judged too harshly. In the words of the Son of Sirach commonly called Ecclesiasticus " Let me entreat you therefore to read it with favour and attention and to pardon us wherein we may seem to come short of some words in that which we have laboured to interpret."

I submit the result to all who love Monmouthshire and its History.

A. P.

Garth, 1946.

CHAPTER I.

THE MYSTERIOUS NAME OF BASSALEG.

"WHY" asked my English friend "why on earth must you live in a place with a name like that ? I can't even pronounce it, let alone spell it," he snorted violently. "That's just typical of Wales."

"That is just where you display your colossal ignorance," I said severely. "For it is not a Welsh name on the other hand I grant you that it isn't English."

"Well, it beats me," he replied "it doesn't seem to mean anything." So I told him it had beaten better men than he—which was no more than the truth.

The origin and derivation of the word "Bassaleg" has been the subject of much discussion and several philologists have had to confess themselves at a loss, or have been content with citing the possibilities and drawing no conclusion. The Reverend James Johnston, in his "Place names of England and Wales,¹" concluded his paragraph on Bassaleg by saying "The present Welsh pronounciation varies between Maesaleg, Maeshalyg (field of willows) and Maesholwg (said to be a Salt Field) showing that the natives are all at sea, and the rest of us are not much better."!

In the last few years, however, investigation has been rather more scientific with the result that the deriviation of the name has become reasonably certain.

My Englishman was right in some ways. It is not Welsh nor is it English, it means nothing as it stands

---

(¹London John Murray 1915)

and it is certainly corrupted or derived from something. If the later Welsh writers had not found the word meaningless and unattractive to their ears, accustomed as they were to the lilting descriptiveness of the average Welsh place name, if they had not decided that it must have had a comprehensible and fair-sounding Welsh original, the unfortunate confusion, which caused the Reverend Johnston to give way to such despair, would never have arisen.

Having misread their Dafydd ap Gwilym, they decided regrettably that it was derived from "Maesaleg" and this so caught hold of the minds of the Welsh speaking population that they regarded "Bassaleg" as a bastard anglicization of the order of "Blaina" or "Rumney." In fact they thought it was worse, because it was the root first syllable which had been entirely destroyed. Within living memory a Welshman of Bassaleg has refused to call it any other than Maesaleg when giving evidence in Court. He may be excused for this mistake, since the fallacy achieved large and full-blown proportions and before proceeding to the correct derivation it would be as well to deal with it thoroughly, once and for all.

Dafydd ap Gwilym, the greatest of Welsh poets, of whom I shall have very much more to say in a later chapter, makes two mentions in his poems of the village in which he was living. Both allusions when translated mean " In Bassaleg."

Now the Welsh word " Yn," In, governs what is called the Nasal Mutation. In Welsh grammar there are nine consonants, which change into other consonants, in certain given sets of grammatical circumstances. Six of these have a nasal mutation, which as I have said is governed among other words by " Yn." B happens to be one of them, so that instead of " Yn Bassaleg," in correct Welsh, we write " Ym Massaleg." Professor Ifor Williams has examined the problem and decided that what Dafydd really wrote was "Ym Masaleg" and "Ym Mysaleg," and not "Ym Maesaleg." The one is clearly a mutation of the spelling as we know it to-day, the other, "Bysaleg," is found in its original in M.S. Peniarth 147 in a list of the Cantrefs, Commotes and Parishes of Wales and is a spelling variant on the Bass-root. When this was first demonstrated to the Maesaleg school of thought they retorted that Mas was a likely misspelling of Maes and that as m has no nasal mutation it proved nothing. They did not add that Mys from a familiar word like Maes is a much less likely scribal error.

Ym is not only used instead of Yn before words beginning with a B or P which have mutated to M or Mh but is often written before words beginning originally with M and so is no help to us.

Whatever can be made of this one thing is quite clear. When the first popular edition of Dafydd was printed in London in 1789 both quotations were set down as "Yn Maesaleg." The two men who published it and who were subsequently to bring out the famous "Myfyrian Archaiology of Wales," Owen Jones (known as Myfyr) and William Owen (Pughe), did not scruple to include in the appendix as genuine Dafydd ap Gwilym spurious poems, probably by their acquaintance Edward Williams (Iolo Morganwg). While it is not yet fully determined which of the 287 poems in the 1789 edition are spurious, Professor Williams regards seven at least of the thirteen poems dedicated to Ifor Hael of Gwern y Cleppa in Bassaleg as genuine; among the seven are the two which refer to Bassaleg by name.

From the spelling given in the widely read 1789 edition of Dafydd the idea soon spread that the original Welsh must have been Maesaleg and in the course of the Nineteenth century a variety of meanings were unearthed and foisted upon this inaccurate version. They had no validity whatsoever.

Maeslaeg, we were told, meant the " Field of Alexander or the " Field of Aellog or Aloc." There is a town in Perthshire called Alyth, in an old form Allechtt." It might be " The Field of Allectus," someone else suggested. This quickly developed. "Allectus points to a North British Origin," said the Reverend John Griffith and The Archæologia Cambrensis for the year 1864 declared that it was the Allectus who succeeded Carausius—a man who in 285 A.D. declared Britain independent of Rome and held power for thirteen years. "Allectus was probably defeated in the west at Campus Aelecti or Maesaleg in Monmouthshire."

With the Reverend James Johnston's efforts I have already dealt ! Altogether this was a pretty collection to spring from what was in its origin a baseless fallacy but there was worse to come. In the effort to find a historical background to Maesaleg the unfortunate village found its name verging on to the mythological ; through an unlucky sentence in Nennius we reached the edge of the Arthurian Legend.

I would rather proceed straight away to examine the suggested derivations of the Bass-root and the derivation which is nowadays regarded as correct but the Nennius story is of exceptional interest and is so widely quoted that some may come across it and be confused if I omit discussion of it altogether.

Apart from the Anglo-Saxon Chronicle and Bede there are only two Pre-Conquest sources which purport to give any account of events in Britain after the withdrawal of aid from Rome about 410 A.D. One is Gildas, a monk, who was born in the year of the great Victory over the Saxons at Badon Hill ; in his " De Excidio Britanniæ " (The Destruction of Britain) he first gives some vague account of the events of the 5th century and then proceeds to his condemnation of the sins of the rulers of Britain and the just punishment which has befallen them.   He us tells how King Vortigern (to give his name the popular spelling) invited the Saxons to Britain to help fight the northern Picts and says truly how foolish this was because not unnaturally it proved impossible to get rid of them after the battles were over. Gildas then falls to moaning, preaching and telling of the horrors that befell the disorganised Britons. Suddenly he returns to fact, and describes how they rallied under the direction of one Ambrosius "who alone of all the Roman nation was then left alive," and fought the campaigns leading up to the victory of Mount Badon.

The relevance of all this becomes apparent when we turn to the other historian whose work contains an account of the period—Nennius. Nennius probably lived in South Wales and published his work, the " Historia Britonum " in the first half of the ninth century.   His account of the years when Vortigern called in the Saxons is an expanded version of the events that were related by Gildas.   The accounts tally so well that I would fully accept the conclusion of Mr. T. D. Reed in his brilliant essay published last year* that Nennius was deriving his material from the same source as Gildas, and a trustworthy source at that, if he (Nennius) then did not launch into a fantastic tale of magic in Sections 40-43 of the " Historia."   It is this piece of romance that is supposed to concern Bassaleg.   Roughly what happens is that Vortigern, driven to the rocks of Wales reaches Snowdon and there his Wise Men counsel him to build a fortress which will withstand his Saxon enemies.   Whenever the necessary building materials are collected they are spirited away in the night.   The King calls the Wise Men who say that if he ever wants to get his city built he must kill a child born without a father and sprinkle the ground with its blood.   Messengers are sent throughout the

---

* " Battle for Britain in the 5th Century "—Methuen, 1944

land to find such a child and, lo and behold, a child was found playing ball, whose mother denied that she had ever had anything to do with any man, at " Campus Aelecti " (or Electi, Elleti or Gleti according to manuscript) " which is in the region called Glevising." Glevising or Glywyseg, to which I shall return later, is the region between the rivers Usk in Monmouthshire and Thaw in Glamorgan. "Aleg " we were told, was a corruption of "Aelecti " ; " Campus " is the Latin equivalent of the Welsh " Maes "—in fact Maesaleg !

One might as well finish the Story. The child swiftly solved the problem by unearthing a red and a white serpent under Vortigern's site. The red conquered the white, and the boy said that the King must go away from the place and that the magic serpent or dragon meant that the Red Dragon of Britain would drive the White Dragon of the Saxons into the Sea. " What is your name ? " said the King. "Ambrose," replied the boy, " in Welsh Embresguletic. A Roman Consul was my Father." The King then sets him to rule over the Western Provinces.

To make this incredible tale Nennius has taken the Romano-British Ambrosius Aurelianus out of his proper setting and given him the name of some Welsh enchanter Emrys Wledig. He has taken the flight of the broken Vortigern from his own people and made it a retreat from the Saxons, and lastly he has thrown in a favourite Welsh folk story—the fight of the Red and White Dragons, which is found in another form in the Tale of " Lludd and Llevelys " in the Mabinogion.

The upshot of this farrago of nonsense, provided that it is not an interpolation in the MSS., for which it is certainly rather lengthy, is that it must cast great doubt on Nennius even after Mr. Reed's book, which omits all reference to the passage.

To this story Nennius added in the famous paragraph

50 the account of the victories over the Saxons not of Ambrosius but of Arthur. It only needed the vivid imagination or, if you prefer it, the capacity for falsehood, of Geoffrey of Monmouth to turn the "Ambrose" child into his immortal 12th Century Enchanter Myrddin Emrys or Merlin.

Doubtless the tale has given birth to a good deal more than its author expected. For it is the " Campus Ellecti " of this baseless nonsense that has been quoted as the Latin version of the Welsh Maesaleg—I have already given one example from the Archœlogia Cambrensis. Surely in view of the nature of the tale, of the origin of " Maesaleg " in a misquoting of Dafydd and of what I shall set out below, it is asking a bit too much to expect us to believe it.

Furthermore we need go no further than the Book of Llandaff to discover a far more probable origin for the " Field of Elleti." In the Episcopate of St. Oudoceus, Third Bishop of Llandaff, Meurig ap Tewdrig King of Glamorgan,by way of penance for the slaying of Cynfeddw gave four villages with two hundred and sixteen acres of land to the church. Those villages were " (1) Riugraenauc, (2) Nantavan, (3) That in which Cynfeddw was slain beyond Nantavan, (4) Beyond Nantavan where the King's son committed adultery, from the Marsh of Elleti as far as Nantavan that is the village of Gueberth." Nantavan is supposed to be Llansannor, by Aberthaw and Llanilltyd Fawr* in Glamorganshire, with Llanmaes, not far away providing the " Campus."†

Enough of Maesaleg and its accretion of myth, tradition and false derivation ! It was necessary to scrape it all away before starting on clearer, surer, foundations.

There has never been wanting a school of thought

---

*   called Llantwit Major
†   Wade-Evans " Nennius," S.P.C.K., 1938

which rejected Maesaleg. There have always been those who strove for a derivation from the Bass-root but unfortunately they never hit the right one.

One thing was clear to all. There was an argument which, added to the Dafydd ap Gwilym myth, over-whelmed the " Maesaleg " case. It was realised that the book of Llandaff was compiled about 1130 and that it mentions the name several times, spelling it Bassaleg, Bassalec and Basselec. Furthermore in 1295 and 1314 surveys were taken of the De Clare estates, and it was there spelt Basselec and Basselech. Dafydd ap Gwilym did not write his poetry till the mid fourteenth century. So nearly 250 years before the supposed first writing of " Maesaleg " it was invariably written with a Bass-root. An Anglicization of Maes into Bass would be inconceiv-able by 1130, nothing in the Book of Llandaff suggests that such a change would have been possible. All other evidence supports this. The Monastic grants have it Bassaleg, Leland has it " Pont Besselec over Ebowith," Saxton, Speed and Morden, the map makers, all give " Bassaleg." " Ymassalec," the rationalized mutation, is found twice in MSS. Peniarth, also the form " Massalec." In all, the original root is clearly Bass-.

The efforts to explain Bass-aleg away did not meet with the success of the fatally simple " Maesaleg."

Bassus we were told was a Romano-British personal name, and one must look at the Eglwysi Bassa of the (supposedly) 6th Century poet Llywarch Hen, which was now Baschurch in Shropshire. Doubtless something similar had occurred in the case of Bassaleg. Basing-stoke offered us Bas- again ! The most plausible of all explanations, which Coxe took up, was that the church being dedicated to Saint Basil the name was derived therefrom. Bassaleg it was then decided was Basil's Ley, or Leah,—Leah being the Anglo Saxon for " woodland or clearing." This would have covered the case were it not for the fact that the Book of Llandaff has it "Bassaleg" and the idea of an Anglo Saxon name in this district in 1130 or before is entirely fantastic. If one tries it in Welsh it is no better. Professor Williams points out* that in Welsh, Church names are not made by adding -eg to the name of the Saint. In any case Basil would be a very out of place Saint in South Wales.

No ! The fact is that the order has been reversed. " Basil " is the mistake, not Bassaleg. The trees have been cleared and at last we can see the wood, the word is derived from the late Latin noun " Basilica " !

This was first pointed out by Dr. Kuno Meyer ; and in 1934 Professor Williams set down the theory in such a manner as to leave no longer any reasonable doubt of its correctness. In Greek and Classical Latin Basilica is used for a Royal dwelling or court house but in the Latin of the 4th Century Church it is the word normally used for a religious building erected on the shrine of a Saint or martyr as opposed to Ecclesia, the usual word for a church.

If proof of this distinction is needed we find it in the pages, strangely enough, of Gildas. To make it clear I must quote the original which refers to the recovery of Christianity after the persecution of Diocletian :—
" Renouant Ecclesias ad solum usque destructum Basilicas Sanctum Martyrium fundant, construunt, proficiunt, ut velut victricia signa passim propalant."

" They restore the churches which have been levelled to the ground : they found, construct and complete Basilicas to the Sacred Martyrs and set forth everywhere the signs of their Victory."

Dr. Hugh Williams in his " Gildas " has a note on this passage in which he says that " a Basilica appears as an Assembly Place in the 4th Century. In the 7th century ' Sacrum Gelasianum ' a service is given for

---

*Journal of the Board of Celtic Studies, Nov., 1936

dedicating a new Basilica. The Roman Martyrology calls them ' Concilia Martyrium.' St. Jerome speaks of Basilicæ, Ecclesiæ and Martyrium Conciliabula."

Among the Britons "Basilica" was generally replaced by Merthyr, the Welsh word for a Martyr—as in Merthyr Tydfil and Merthyr Mawr. However, in one case it was not replaced; here Basilica was retained and that was why when Donovan, passing through in 1800, misspelt Bassaleg as " Basileg " he was getting nearer the truth than he knew.

The original has survived in two cases in Ireland, mentioned by Dr. Meyer and Dr. Williams. One is Baisleac a parish church in Co. Roscommon, the other, a diminutive form, Baisleocan, a townland in Kilcronan, Dunkerran, Co. Kerry; Baslec is the Old Irish for Basilica. Bassaleg is the sole surviving example in Wales and England.

Who the particular martyr was, whether he was slain in an early persecution or a later one, possibly the one under Diocletian, we shall never know. Nor shall we ever know whence came the idea of St. Basil as a dedication for the church. Possibly when, at a later date, a church was constructed, the builder took the idea from the surviving name of Basilica attaching, to the Shrine, which had perhaps fallen into decay. It would be pleasant to believe that the Martyr was a man called Basil, and if one may carry fantasy a ltttle further that he was martyred at the same time as Aeron and Julius were slain at Caerleon or Chester. This is, however mere day-dreaming ; we do do not know why a Basilica was erected on the bank above the Ford of the Ebbw, and we never shall.

CHAPTER II.

WENTLLWG BEFORE THE ROMANS.

IN dealing with the history of any one place it must never be forgotten that the period of time during which we have written records of historical events is very much shorter than the period for which we have no recorded evidence at all. Briefly, one may say that recorded history of Britain opens with the arrival of the Romans. Before that the story of Bassaleg like anywhere else rests not in the hands of the historian but of the archæologist—the man who has to dig in the ground for his information.

The world is infinitely old, many millions of years, and man has been in these islands for less than 17000 of them. Between 15000 and 10000 B.C. the climate of Britain became much warmer, and, as the Glaciers retreated, man advanced. His remains, his workings in bone and ivory, the bones of the mammoth and the woolly rhinoceros, the later elk, cave bear, hyæna and wolf are found in caves off the Pembrokeshire coast, together with the flint cores and chippings resulting from man's efforts at fashioning implements. From these solitary locations of the Paleolithic or Old Stone Age there grew the primitive communities of the period of the Middle Stone Age. Between 8000 B.C. and 4000 B.C. the climate became stabilized, and Britain once and for all became an island.

In the warm countries of the Eastern Mediterranean there grew up a higher form of life ; Ancient Babylon and Egypt developed trade, cities, the acquisition of

wealth and presently there came to the shores of the
Western Islands, ringed by the booming Atlantic surf,
ships bearing traders in search of metals, ships manned
by people from far Iberia, short, dark people who made
landfall on the coasts of Britain, found it a pleasant
country and so remained.   Between 2500 and 2000 B.C.
there followed waves of these folk from the countries
where they had multiplied and spread.   The New Stone
Age had come to Wales.

From here begins the continuous overall inhabitation
of Britain.   From here, Bassaleg and many other places
came into evidence for the first time.   These short,
dark people, with the long narrow heads, from whom in
physical appearance are descended the majority of modern
South Welshmen were no "Ancient Britons " living in
caves.   They built hut settlements, they pastured cattle,
and they cultivated the hill slopes of Southern England
with a reasonably efficient form of agriculture.   Their
pottery was functional if not beautiful, their weapons
were of flint, mined on the South Downs, or made in
a great factory at Craig Llwyd in North Wales.   Most
striking of all is the regularity size, and organisation
of their burial chambers.   There are plenty of these in
Wales, mostly made up of several large stones giving a
single chamber covered by the usual long shaped mound
or barrow.   Generally the earth has been worn away in
the course of time leaving the stone collapsed or upright;
these are the familiar " Cromlechs " which are
scattered all around the coasts of Wales.   These are
the Megaliths, the Standing Stones that the ignorance
of previous centuries took to be " Druids' Altars."
Bassaleg alone in Wentllwg has vestiges of a long cairn
grave of the New Stone Age period.   It lies just above
the Cardiff Road.   Go from Bassaleg over Cwrt y Defaid,
go through Gwern y Cleppa till you are above the
fishpond below Cefn Llogell Plantation, go due east to

an old barn and a stone wall against the last fields before the Cardiff Road. There are some small quarrying pits by the trees and a mound of waste earth. Some yards away towards Tredegar in the middle of the field are a few large stones and an uneven surface to the ground. This was the communal grave of the first men of Wentllwg. It is scheduled by the Office of Works but has never been excavated, so there is nothing more that can be said about it yet. The nearest neighbours appear to have lived at Portskewett.

The Bronze Age people, a more rugged race than their predecessors, spread in successive uneven waves over these islands between 2000 B.C. and 1000 B.C., and their culture continued to develop down to 500 B.C. The art of working bronze was latterly brought to a magnificent pitch of perfection both in weapon and ornament alike. As for their religious and burial customs, it is to the Early Bronze Age people that we owe the first period of our great national monument of Stonehenge, most of the stone for which was brought from distant Pembrokeshire—an almost incredible feat, speaking of a high degree of religious organisation. The stone which gave its name to Druidstone between Bassaleg and St. Mellons was probably a standing stone of this period. The Bronze Age tomb was a round-shaped mound of earth in marked contrast to the Neolithic Long Cairn.

With its over-carpet of lush forest, steaming hot in summer, full of swamps and wild animals, Bassaleg, naturally, was not a popular place in which to live during the Bronze Age. The nearest Round Barrow, Twyn Panteg, is situated just off the road from Lower Machen to Pontymister where the lane from Rhiwderin joins it above Coed Mawr. There is another on the summit of Mynydd Machen, one or more on and near Mynydd y Grug and Twyn Cae Hugh above Bedwas, and yet another and possibly more, between Cwrt Henllys and the top of Twyn Barllwm, situated on a level plateau about half way up the hillside. In Bassaleg itself we know of nothing. The hut settlements, the storehouses and the miserable hill pastures of these people must, in varying degrees of concentration, have clung sparsely to our hillsides for more than a thousand years.

This was very different from the Wentllwg of the Iron Age—the period which in Britain lasts from approximately 500 B.C. to the Roman invasion. Bassaleg at the end of this time seems to have had a population quite as numerous as it had in any period up to the nineteenth century. These people no longer dwelt in hut settlements but in and around hill forts ; it is probable that they maintained a tradition of Bronze Age culture till the last century before Christ, for iron working came late into Wales.

The hill forts which are characteristic of Iron Age settlements are found in great numbers all over Britain and nowhere thicker than along the coast of South Wales. Successive waves of Celtic peoples were driven westward from Europe and each one retired to hill forts as a defence against the next.

These hill forts are an everyday part of the landscape in Bassaleg, overlooked as it is by the colossal ramparts of Gaer (Tredegar Golf Course) and by the plantation on Cwrt y Defaid hill. If you study a map of Iron Age Wales you will see that there are several concentrations of hill camps, one of which lies between Chepstow and Cardiff. The centre of this is between St. Julian's and St. Mellons and the most populous place of all is Bassaleg. There are no less than five hill forts in Bassaleg : Tredegar Fort, Cwrt y Defaid, Pen-y-lan, Croes Carn Einion and Rhiwderin. They look simple enough now, mere grassy mounds, but when they were built they were a formidable enough obstacle to any invading force.

IRON AGE FORT AT
CRAIG Y SAESON.
(Reconstructed)

M. EDMONDS

It is so easy to imagine them as they were, the castles and the pill-boxes of their day. The ditches surrounding the ringed banks were deep cut, straight down into the red earth, the walls supported and backed by timber facings. Beyond the ditch was a bare foothold and then the sheer face of the wooden rampart. Behind this lay the earth that had been dug out of the ditch, piled high and stamped firmly into a solid bank; giving complete protection. The entrance was set well back between the banks so that no attacker could live in the narrow approach let alone scale the stout wooden barrier. Who cannot see in the mind's eye the sentry's warning of suspicious movements down by the Ebbw, or hear the call to arms, the heat and clash of battle, the cries of the broken attackers driven down the hill by a victorious sally ? Who cannot imagine the corpses of the slain lying speared in the ditch ?

Yes, formidable enough to capture with spear and sword and, when confronted with a truly gigantic earthwork such as Tredegar Fort, an impossible task for anything short of a large army. Tredegar Fort is a fine example of an Iron Age stronghold ; it has not been subject to the ravages of the plough, its ditches are still deep and formidable. If it were only excavated on a large scale, our knowledge of the Iron Age in this area would be considerably expanded, and possibly not only that of the Iron Age. Many of these forts were, in England, refortified in the period following the departure of the Romans as a defence against a large number of invasions from various quarters ; very much the same thing may have happened on the coast of South Wales. Archæologists however have a colossal task before them, and Iron Age forts must wait their turn. The only one in Monmouthshire that has been " dug " is the great Llanmelin Camp above the Roman City of Caerwent. Still Tredegar's double and triple ramparts are firm enough. They can afford to wait awhile longer.

On the opposite hill to Tredegar Fort, on the other side of the Ebbw is another Gaer. Nowadays it is called Cwrt y Defaid, the Court of Sheep, but when Archdeacon William Coxe came through Monmouthshire in 1789 it was known by the name which is now given only to the farm on the further slope—Graig y Saeson. Now Saeson can mean either a Saxon, an Englishman or a foreigner and needless to say, we do not know why this particular example of Iron Age defensive ring-working should have received such a title. When it is excavated we shall perhaps find that it was refortified by the local inhabitants after the Romans departed and the coast was defenceless against raids by Saxon sea pirates ; perhaps we shall discover that the foreigners actually assaulted and took the fort ; but it is just as likely that at some time in the Middle Ages somebody came to the profoundly inaccurate conclusion that these forts had been originally constructed by Germanic invaders and that the name caught on from there. As it happens, similar names are to be found in other parts of South Wales, mostly on the edge of the fertile lowlands that formed the target for all hostile incursions century after century ; it is fruitless to speculate on their origins.

Coxe speaks of Cwrt y Defaid as being thickly over-grown with trees, and it was only in recent years that these gave place to a close plantation of larch. Although a mere single ringwork and very much smaller than its giant neighbour on the Eastern hill it presents features of great interest. The trees have spared it the levelling influence of the plough and it is here that we can best visualize the deep ditch and the towering bank topped by the palisade. It was always possible to increase these obstacles by placing unpleasantly sharp stakes in the ditch on which the impetuous attacker, slipping in his assault, might be impaled.

I have never believed that all the dwellings of an Iron
Age settlement could have been sited in the central space
of these small ring works.   Somewhere on the sunny
southern slope of Cwrt y Defaid, not so very far
above the spot where 2000 years before the men of
Neolithic Bassaleg had buried their dead, there must
have been a cluster of Iron Age dwellings, barns and
workshops.   Then at the call of danger, the women and
children, flocks and herds, would be secured within the
ramparts, while the men set the place in a state of prepared defence.

The Cwrt y Defaid Fort has an exceptionally well
preserved entrance.   The modern ride through the wood
enters the Fort on the Newport side, actually through
the original gateway.   On the attackers' right, the spear
side, the bank thickness at the gate terminal turned
inwards.   Sir Cyril Fox is of the opinion that, on the
club end so formed, there stood a tower or platform
of wood, so that any attacker reaching the gateway came
under direct point blank fire from a superior position.
He was doubly vulnerable as the defending arrows came
in on his open side, his shield thus affording him no
protection.   It is 27 feet across that terminal so that
there was ample space for a sizeable structure.   The
defences where the terminal joins the bank must have
been a good 14 yards across, from the outer edge of the
ditch to the top of the inner ramp Below the woodland
ride, leading out of the ditch is a clear hollow way.
This would be the road of approach to the main gate
and in point of fact it also leads down to a spring—the
water supply of the defenders.   There was only one
entrance to the stockade—the turned one ; the modern
ride, where it leaves the wood on the Western side,
breaks through the old mound and ditch.   At this point
the original base of the heaped wall can be clearly seen,
marked off by a line of rabbit holes, for rabbits and

foxes always start their buries in the softer man-heaped soil of an earth bank rather than in the solid cut sides of a ditch.

Of about the same size as Cwrt y Defaid was the third " encampment " mentioned by Coxe. Pen y Parc Newydd Gaer lies in a small field just to the Channel side of Pen y lan hamlet. It can be easily distinguished by an Ordnance Survey Triangulation Stone in the middle. Coxe marks an entrance at the South Western corner but the whole thing is so ploughed in that it is difficult to say anything definite about it.

There were two more Iron Age Communities in our area. Coxe can be forgiven for missing them since they are in such a state as to be barely recognisable as single ring works at all. One lies on the Bassaleg side of the drive leading from the Michaelstone road to Croes Carn Einion Farm. There is a barely visible segment of ring ditch—at least it is difficult to account for it as anything but that.

The other is more obvious. It lies on the bluff overlooking the Ebbw, 200 yards from the end of Rhiwderin Street in the direction of the Castle Works. The other edge of the Work has been ploughed down the hill but from the railway or Garth Corner a long segment is clearly visible running in an angle between two hedges. Some energetic probing for bed rock or hard earth would doubtless reveal the extent of the ditch.

It may be fanciful, it may be pure chance, but it is worth noting that there is a remarkable degree of visual intercommunication between these ring-works. From Cwrt y Defaid they are all visible—the Rhiwderin one just appears in the edge of the Garth Cutting. Pen y Parc is the only exception, and the people there would have had to come barely as far as Prospect Cottage to see all the others,—in fact a smoke signal would have been plainly visible.

These Iron Age Forts did not lack neighbours. There were some above Cefn Mably, there were some at Pont Hir, at St. Julian, at Kemeys Folly, above Penhow and Llanvaches ; they had their capital at Llanmelin and so away over the hilltops to Trellech their Forts were dotted. These forts date from the Silures of Tacitus—a numerous race, even if the Roman author exaggerates their number. These were a mixed stock of Neolithic and Bronze Age peoples, short and sturdy, long headed and dark, speaking a tongue not unlike modern Welsh. A Celtic people from the South West of England who had intermarried with them to some extent, had taught them to build Hill Forts. Around these they practised an agricultural economy and an unpleasant religion of great efficiency run by Druids from North Wales, involving human sacrifice to the strange Celtic gods.

These were the people who in the summer of the year of our Lord 43 learnt that Claudius, the Emperor of Rome, had invaded England with 40,000 men.

CHAPTER III.

ROMANS AND ROADS.

THE Silures battled hard and desperately. One wonders how many of the men of Bassaleg left home to fight the invaders and to take part in raids often as far as the Fosse way in Gloucestershire; how many fought with their great national leader Caractacus in his last great fight in Powysland; how many sacked Gloucester while the Romans had trouble both in the east with Queen Boadicea and to the north with the tribes of Brigantia. One wonders also how many ever again saw their hill forts above the Ebbw.

It was fully thirty-five years after Claudius landed that the brave people of South Wales were subdued and with them the last hope of the Britons was gone. The Governor of Britain, Frontinus, conquered South and Mid Wales between 74 and 77 A.D. and within a year or two he and his equally energetic successor, Agricola, had set up the system of military government of Wales that was to last for 300 years.

The two pivotal points of the system were the Legionary headquarters of the II Augusta at Isca (Caerleon) and XX Victrix at Deva (Chester). From each of these spread a network of roads and subsidiary fortresses—such as Abergavenny, Usk and Gelligaer.

The Roman Government of Wales was purely military. In only one place did Frontinus construct a civil town on the model of Bath, London or Silchester—this was at Venta Silurum (Caerwent). It was wise, since the attraction of a civilised town with baths and a theatre

soon brought the Silures out of their Capital, the Iron
Age Fort on Llanmelin Hill. To the rest of South
Wales, and to Bassaleg, the Roman soldiers made no
more difference than the British garrisons on the North
West Frontier of India make a difference in the lives of
the hill tribes of that equally far flung corner of another
Empire. The men of Bassaleg carried on. very likely,
in their old hill forts or just outside them, with the old
pursuits of pasture and hill cultivation. They still wore
rough woven clothes but if a cooking pot, or a spear
or an ornamental vase appeared over the hearth, stamped
with the trade mark of some factory on the far away
Rhine, then it was only because some member of the
family had gone for a day's outing to the shops of Caerwent, had a bath, been to a show, and returned to Cwrt
y Defaid rather late at night, for all the world like his
modern descendant coming up Pentrepoeth after missing
the last bus from Cardiff !

Although the Romans did not develop in South Wales
a country squirearchy dwelling in luxurious villas on
extensive estates as they did in the Cotswolds, they still
needed roads, good roads, to link up their military
outposts. Trunk roads were amenities of civilization
scarcely within the range of the pre-Roman organisation.

When G. K. Chesterton wrote :—
" Before the Roman came to Rye And out to Severn
    strode "
" The Rolling English drunkard built the rolling English
    road,"
he was only partly correct. On the dry chalk uplands
of Southern England were the ancient trodden ways,
along which moved all the major Folk migrations and
some traffic, but in South Wales it was a different matter.
The deep valleys were choked with oak forest making
lateral communication almost impossible, except in the
marshy coastal plain. Between the Hill Forts of the

first ridges there were forest tracks, uncertain lanes through the vegetation, where lurked the wild boar and the wolf, but in the hinterland the deep valleys were often uncrossable.

From an Ordnance Map of to-day it can be seen that the roads of North West Monmouthshire run in deep parallel valleys, now cleared of their undergrowth. Follow the ridges from North to South and there is generally a traceable footpath, fragment of a lane that begins and ends nowhere in particular, or sometimes part of a modern second class road; as like as not there is a Round Barrow or camp every few miles. These are the lines of the Bronze Age roads and inhabited sites of the pre-Roman period, and these roads continued in use throughout the Middle Ages. It is easy to see why the earliest villages Bedwellty, Gelligaer, and Mynyddislwyn, were set high on the mountain far above the industrial settlements on the valley floor which sprang up only when the forests were cleared in the 18th century.

Such was the road " system " which the Romans found and to a people who needed above all things a means of switching troops with great rapidity from one position to another it was of very little use. So within a few years they extended the Via Julia Maritima from Aquae Solis (Bath) to the Severn, just above Avonmouth. From there the passage was made to Portskewett, or thereabouts, and the road entered the new Forum at Caerwent. Passing thence over Cats Ash the highway dropped down to the bridge and so across the river to the great fortress of Isca. Northward from Isca the border road ran up through Usk (Burrium) and Abergavenny (Gobannium) to Kentchester, Leintwardine, and so on via Wroxeter (Vriconium) to the other great legionary headquarters, the other Caerlleon, Deva (Chester).

In the other direction the Via Julia carried on to

Cardiff, Nidum (Neath), Leucarum (Llwchwr), and
to Maridunum (Carmarthen).

For our purpose the all important stretch of the great
road is the one from Caerleon to Cardiff, and unfortunately we can nowhere be sure of its exact course.

Coxe said that it started under the Lodge Camp
proceeding straight between Malpas Church and Crindau
House, where it is lost among the canal works. Then
he makes it swing crazily down to St. Woolos. " The
course from hence towards the Taff is doubtful as the
present road divides into two branches which unite at
St. Mellons, the Upper goes by Bassaleg, the lower by
Tredegar and Castleton. The chain of encampments I
(Coxe) have described are equally calculated to defend
both." In point of fact the Hill Forts were built at
least two hundred years before the Roman Road, a
reflection of the complete ignorance of archæology
existing until quite recent times.

Mr. F. J. Hando is in full agreement with this route
as far as Barrack Lane and then he suggests that it leads
straight over Ridgeway and down through Bassaleg.
From Bassaleg he follows it over Pen y Lan, into
Glamorgan, on to the top of Cowbridge Common and
so to the West. In his opinion the road is prehistoric,
starting from the Lodge Camp (" Belinstoke ")—which
was probably another Iron Age hill fort.

I am not prepared to state with certainty that there
was a pre-Roman track but whoever first built an inland
road must have taken precisely this line of clear ridges.
This is the obvious route by which to enter South Wales
and has been throughout the Ages.

Granting without further argument that in some
fashion, the road came over Ridgeway and went up to
Pen y lan, nothing more definite is known about its
course. The one inch Ordnance Map is careful not to
mark a " Roman Road " at all. The six inch map is

not so cautious. It bows to local opinion and marks the Roman Road in bold type but even then with a timid " Supposed " in Italics before it. This " supposed' stretch of road runs in the hollow through the garden of Prospect Cottage, follows the modern road and swings under the trees in the steep part of the hill.

At the right handed bend the hollow was very deep up to a few years ago but it is now filled with road rubbish. From the big tree at the entrance to Croesheolydd drive there is a barely discernable depression in the field running parallel with the modern road. Near the marsh we have to suppose, if tradition and the six inch map are to be upheld, that the road turned to the left over a clearly defined raised pathway, and then to the right into the sand pit. From there a hollow way follows the twists and turns of the hedge, past Fynnon Oer barn, down to the Bassaleg Brook.

I am prepared to admit the Roman possibilities of the first two hundred yards below Prospect Cottage ; there is a chance for the depression in the field but I reject the section on the hill where the road and hollow way bend slightly to the right and I am sorry to say that I damn completely the whole winding stretch from the marsh, through Pool Sands down the hedge to Bassaleg Brook.

The Roman road builders made corners only where it was absolutely necessary, for the turning of a corner, suitable for a really fast military road, needs cambering and drainage. This takes much valuable time, and speed was the whole secret of the Romans' complete success in military movement. Therefore a bend between the river and Pen y lan top would be quite inadmissible which excludes both the slight bend in the present hollow way and the whole twisting track of the lower section. We cannot suppose that a people concerned with getting to and from Caerleon on the straightest possible course would swing aside to pass through what is now Pentrepoeth, when there lay, on the direct route, a clean gentle slope down to the Ebbw. As a sop to outraged feelings I will say that at one time there has been a track the whole way up and that the whole section from the Croesheolydd drive to Prospect Cottage has been a sunken mediæval pack way ; but I think that the lower half running under the hedge to Pentrepoeth so far from being Roman or mediæval, is nothing more or less than the original tram or cart road down which sand was brought from Pool Sands Pit to the Iron Forge that stood in Tredegar Park in the 18th Century.

I have hopes of two sections of the " supposed Roman Road." Some work with an iron probe would probably produce good results ; but it is unfortunately true that we do not know how the Roman Road got down to the Ebbw or at what point the river was crossed. Let us be honest with ourselves. The course of the Via Julia Maritima where it passed through Bassaleg is irretrievably lost.

Before leaving the Roman period there is one other matter to be discussed. The Romans were very interested in the mineral wealth of Wales. Besides the well known gold mine at Dolaucothi they obtained copper, iron and coal from different parts of the country. In addition there was lead. This was mined mostly in North Wales but an important section of the Imperial lead mines had its headquarters at Lower Machen to exploit the mineral wealth of Coed Cefn Pwll Du. During the construction of the new road in 1936-37 sufficient pottery was found, together with a fragment of capital, to indicate that there had been a Roman settlement, probably on the site of the present village.*

---

* See Arch. Camb. 1936 for previous discoveries of coins in and above Draethen and the Journal of the Board of Celtic Studies, 1937-38, p. 395, for Dr. Nash Williams' Article on the discoveries made during the construction of the new road.

There would have been a slave barracks and offices and
at least one substantial stone building to house the
officers, overseers and guards.   The miners were either
slaves, war prisoners or convicts, for Roman criminals
were, if not executed, condemned to forced labour in
the state mines.   Where was the road to this Settlement ?
I suggest that it either left the Via Julia on Ridgeway,
crossed the Ebbw below Rhiwderin and then went to
Lower Machen by the usual way or else, and much more
likely, because it would avoid a second river crossing,
that it left the main highway on top of Pen y lan and went
straight through Park Wood over the meadows to Lower
Machen.   This is far the simplest and shortest route
for a side road from Lower Machen to take, in order to
join the main thoroughfare.   There is a distinct hollow
way and track in Park Wood crossing the Park House
brook fifty yards from the Rhymni bank.   It is heading
for Lower Machen from the Pen y lan direction and
can be traced for several hundred yards, losing itself on
the edge of the plough-land called Old England above
the Hanging Cover.   This Way, which in one place still
runs between two banks and has till recently been hidden
in a fir plantation, is always supposed to be a continuation
of the disused lane running from Pen y Groes Fach
through Clearwell to the Michaelstone Road below
Holly House.   One is always told that that lane is "An
old coach road to Lower Machen, carrying on in Park
Wood " but I am inclined to think that it was simply
a farm track and that the hollow way in Park Wood,
or anyway its site, is something quite different and
possibly a good 1800 years older.

CHAPTER IV.

THE DARK AGES AND CHRISTIANITY.

THE ensuing period which lasted no less than six hundred years, up to the Norman Conquest, is a dull one. In South Wales it is darker than in most places and what little information we have is exceedingly patchy and uninteresting.

The Second Legion was withdrawn about 383 to Richborough to defend the Eastern shore against Saxon pirates and twenty-seven years later Honorius, the Roman Emperor, hiding in the marshes of Ravenna from the barbarous onslaught, rejected the appeal for military aid from the Romano-British Administration. This is no place to discuss the utter chaos of history and historical sources in the ensuing two hundred years. Wentllwg was too far East for the Irish Invasions, too far South for the Picts. For a time at least it was too far West to be affected by the Saxons. The Battles of Arthur and Ambrosius in England, even the victory of Liddington Hill* (Mount Badon) in 497, could have had little effect. However, after the battle of Deorham (near Bath) in 577 the Saxons entered Gloucester, so Wales was cut off from the South West. Later, in 613 at Chester and in 655 at Winwaed Field, the North was similarly severed. Henceforth England was under Anglo-Saxon control while the Roman-Britains in Cornwall, Wales and Cumberland were separated from each other for ever. In Wales native Princes speedily reappeared after the Legions departed. Myth, literature, legend and chronicle play with the names of Maelgwn Gwynedd,

---

* I accept absolutely Mr. T. D. Reed's conclusions as to the whereabouts of the much disputed site of the famous battle.

Cadwallon, and Cunedda, but since, in the early part of the period, " Wales " stretched as far as Edinburgh, the task of localising any given place name is made very difficult. For example the same name might well be used for Caerleon, Chester or Carlisle.

The one certain factor was the Celtic Church. Although until the arrival of Augustine, Roman Christianity in England was extinguished, the Celtic Church, founded probably in the Second Century by Roman traders and soldiers and now cut off from direct communication with Rome, survived on its own, linked up across the sea with the Goidelic Church in Ireland.

The Institutions of Welsh Christianity, and, presumably, the worship at a certain Basilica on the Ebbw, were kept up through the shining energy of Saints such as Illtyd, Teilo, and the great Dewi, the Patron Saint of Wales himself. The Celtic Church returned to Rome strengthened from its trials on Easter Day 768.

Offa's Dyke was built about 760-785, and from the middle of the Eighth Century Wales assumed finally her traditional division into Kingdoms, Cantrefs, Cwmwds and Trefs. No two lists of these ever agree exactly ; their boundaries are never certain and they altered from time to time. In South-East Wales one can rarely be sure when any given cantref was united to its neighbour or when both were separate, but perhaps ruled over by different branches of the same family.

Although South Wales was officially the Kingdom of Deheubarth, in practice the Eastern and Western halves, Morganwg and Dyfed, were nearly always separate.

The Eastern Cantref of Morganwg was called Gwent ; it was usually sub-divided into at least two smaller cantrefs, Gwent Iscoed and Gwent Uwchcoed and sometimes—possibly after a particularly successful season —the Forest of Dean area, known as Cantref Coch, was claimed as well. As often as not we find Gwent to be a separate principality lorded over by a branch of the ruling family of Morganwg.

The Western cantref of Morganwg was called Glywyseg, later referred to as Glevising; and its boundaries are supposed to have been the Rivers Usk and Thaw. Traditionally it was founded in the Sixth Century by one Glywys but whether this is true or not it was held in 630 along with Gwent by one Meurig ap Tewdrig whom we encountered in the first chapter of this book. Meurig was succeeded about 700 by Morgan Mwynfawr who is supposed to have given his name to Glamorgan, Gwlad Forgan, Morganwg—or what you will. From then onwards our part of South Wales is ruled by a dynasty of whom varying pedigrees are given and varying tales told—not very interesting ones—in a number of Welsh records.

It is of greater interest to us that Glywys is said to have had a son Gwynllyw who founded the great church site of St. Gwynllyw's (corrupted to St. Woolos) at what later became Newport. This may or may not be so, but we are also told that the same Gwynllyw gave his name to the Eastern portion of Glywyseg, the sub-cantref that lay between the Rhymni and the Usk, the area that was later called the Hundred of Wentlooge. This is almost certainly incorrect. The word Gwent is older than we know for the Romans took it in order to name their new civil town—Venta—and when they had gone it was again named or renamed—Caerwent. Gwent Uwchcoed and Gwent Iscoed, Gwent Above and Gwent Below the Forest; those were the names of the two Cantrefs of Gwent. Is it not more reasonable to suppose that Wentlooge has some essentially similar origin? I have called it Wentllwg in this book. It is as good a way of spelling it as any other.*

---

* The word " Gwenlly " in Pillgwenlly is either derived from this name or, if he existed, from Gwynllyw.

It would have been well indeed for the inhabitants of the district if they had retained the virile fighting characteristics of their remote ancestry and had continued to live in the hill forts.   As it was the coast was easy game for the Norsemen.   They were held off in Gwynedd and Powys by the great Welsh Kings Rhodri Mawr and Hwyel Dda, but in the more independent South-Eastern corners of Wales there was no rescue.   Although in 893 the savage pagan invaders were defeated at Tidenham, near Chepstow, by the Gwentian men in alliance with Alfred the Great and the Saxons, they appeared once again after a break of only three years, coming in 896 from Northern and Eastern England and ravaging all South Wales.   In 915 the terrible Long Ships sailed into the Usk Mouth, and the raiders plundered all Gwent capturing the Bishop of Llandaff.   Sporadic terror raids of varying strength continued at intervals for the next two and a half centuries, leaving us with names such as Skomer and Flat Holm for the islands around our coast.

Till about 850 the descendants of Morgan ruled in Gwent and Glywyseg when the latter fell into the hands of one Hywel ap Rhys.   There were a number of unedifying family quarrels and murders and when when the last independent King of Gwent died, all Morganwg—a name which was now used to signify only the older Glywyseg—was united with Gwent and the rest of Wales under the great Gruffydd ap Llewelyn. Gruffydd was slain in 1063 so that there was little time for Wales to break out into warring kingdoms again before, in 1066, the event occurred on Senlac Hill above Hastings, which was in a few years to put an end to this lengthy and ill documented period of history not only in England but throughout South Wales.

CHAPTER V.

ROGERSTONE CASTLE AND BASSALEG PRIORY

SO the leading parish of Wentllwg awaited its conqueror and while it waited there appeared the first priest fo the parish whose name is preserved to us. The Book of Llandaff says " Caradoc, King of Glamorgan* sent some of his household to Llanmocha which belonged to St. Dubricius, St. Teilo, St. Oudoceus and Bishop Herwald, who partook of a banquet prepared by the Bishop without consent of his guest Rhydderch ap Egwyd, and afterwards forcibly remained all night overpowered and intoxicated with much liquor." The king submitted to the Bishop's wrath and did penance at Llandaff. Then he granted " to God and all Bishops of Llandaff for ever the village of Tref Rita in Edelicion† by Merthyr Tecmed‡ with all its liberty in fields, in woods and in pastures, and with all Commonage to be given to the inhabitants." There were a number of witnesses, ecclesiastical and lay, among them Bishop Herwald, King Caradoc and " Benedictus the Priest, of Bassalec."

"A Blessing on him who will preserve this alms in peace for the service of Llandaff, and a malediction with perpetual curse on anyone who by force or fraud shall separate it from the Church of Llandaff. Amen."

In 1037 the dread giants from the Northern Seas and the Western Islands of Scotland descended once

---

* Caradoc ap Rhydderch at Jestyn became King of Morgannwg in 1069 and died in 1070. ‡ Merthyr Tecmed is probably Llandegfedd above Caerleon.
† Edeligion was supposed to be a nebulous district of Central Monmouthshire.

again, but there was to be no more plundering. In 1091
Robert Fitzhamon, follower of Duke William of Normandy, overran South Wales and planted it with his
henchmen. And now the decayed Welsh organization
was gone for ever from Gwent and Morganwg. The
mediæval feudalism—the organization based on Church,
Lord, tenant, sub-tenant and serf took its place.

The Normans spread swiftly westward and Motte and
Bailey Castles sprang up all down the plain and into
the Vale of Glamorgan. The further they went the
longer grew their line of communication and of course
at this point it was dangerously narrow, since the Welsh
were still in control of the hinterland.

It was probably to protect this life line back to
England that the decision was made to refortify the
highest point of the western end of Mynydd Henllys.
It had been a defence point in pre-historic times but
to what extent the Welsh had been using it we do not
know. At any rate when the Normans had finished
their work the resulting mound was of gigantic size,
commanding a view of the whole roof of South Wales.
Succeeding centuries saw this great excrescence on the
hillside and decided that it was pre-historic—that it was
the grave mound of some great chief—in fact, as Arthur
Machen put it, that it was " a mystic tumulus." It
was a grievous blow when modern historical and
archæological opinion came to the conclusion that it was
nothing more than a strategically placed Norman Watch
Tower. Twyn Barllwm had somehow become part of
local faith in a magical past. If anyone still cares to
dispute this let them look at Professor William Rees'
magnificent map series " South Wales and the Border
in the 14th century." Twyn Barllwm is there marked
as a " Castle Site abandoned by the 14th century."
If anyone still wishes to say that it is something else
the onus of proof is henceforward on them ; the mound

is of no recognizable pre-historic type, and if it is not pre-historic what could it be but a motte castle ?

The Norman lord of Bassaleg was Robert of Haia, but within a few years he decided that this was a part of his dominion which could well be spared for pious uses.   Therefore in 1101 occurred one of the most significant events in the history of Bassaleg.   Robert of Haia gave to God and the Abbey of the Blessed Saint Mary at Glastonbury the church of Bassaleg.

He did it in these words

" I Robertus de Haia and my Wife Gundreda, of the lands granted to me by my overlord Robert FitzHamon and his Wife Sibill for the good of our Souls and the Souls of our Ancestors and Descendents do grant to God and the Abbey of Saint Mary at Glastonbury, possession in perpetual Frankalmoign Tenure, free of all Reliefs, Aids, Gelds and other Feudal Burdens, the Church of Bassaleg.   We give it for ever with all its woods, meadows and streams and this we do in order that we may obtain the Blessing and Prayers of the Community.   We also give to the Abbey of Glastonbury the Churches which belong to Bassaleg, that is to say the Churches of Mauhayn, Bedewas, Menedwiscelyn, and Mapmoil, also the Chapel of Coittarnen and the Chapel of Pulcred.   These we give with their tithes, dues and their burial grounds.   And lest any dispute or scandalous argument (which God forbid) should arise between Bassaleg and its neighbouring parishes concerning the Parish Boundaries it is our desire that these boundaries should be set out in English in order that they may be understood by the local inhabitants.   The Parish of Bassaleg begins at St. Cadoc's fountain . . . "

The grant here lapses into a curious dialect of Old English.   One would scarcely have supposed that Anglo-Saxon was any more intelligible than Latin to the Gwentian Welsh and it seems a strange way of making things clear. It mentions names such as Pencarn, New Ebboth, Ebboth, Tenbrith and Dufeles and goes on, still in Old English—" . . . and so to the Broad Stone and so in to Remni and so to Henbon and so to Inweri and so to Inperi and so to Namelin and the Mountains of Sunlinch, to Rid Cambrem and on to Kemeli and so back down to Radoke's Pool." Then it resumes in Latin.

" We give also to Glastonbury one part of our land which is in the Marsh and these are its boundaries :— from the ford at Merepul to Kemelin and on to Elboth, an area of four Hams of land extending as far as the pool called Kenerad and from Kenerad Pool to a little wash of water among the thorn bushes, and from there back to Merepul.

" Also we grant to the monks as much of our woods as is necessary for them, to hold in undisturbed possession free from all feudal and customary suits and services ; and in these woods they may have the right of pasturing their hogs without paying to me the customary payment for the right of swine-feeding that is called Pannage.

"Also the monks are to have all the fishing rights, for a stretch of the Elboth runs through (or by)* one part of their land, and in addition to this they are to have the right of cutting wood from the place that is called Az Dormanz to the spring that is called Contra Werthin, and from there to Stanhus through the rushes to Penbur and so back to the river Elboth.

" To the monks of Glastonbury who will live at Bassaleg we will give of our charity twenty shillings a year to provide their clothing and this sum is to be drawn out of the tithe of Gunleonc.†

"Also we give them our servant Wighi the son of Wrgan together with his land held in free tenure that

---

* influit
† Gunleonc—the district as known as Wentllyg.

he may serve them. And if any of my men, French, English or Welsh wishes to join himself and his land to the monastery or to give land to it then before God he has my permission to do so."

To this document there were a number of witnesses, among them Herlewin the Abbot of Glastonbury, and very soon after the Abbey must have sent a number of the brethren to found the new community. The exact size of their estate we shall never know, but the mention of Pencarn and the river Ebbw, also the churches of Bedwas, Machen, Mynyddislwyn, and the chapel of what appears to be Coedkernew, show us that it was no inconsiderable acquisition.

The rest of these names, including those of the " Church of Mapmoil " and the " Chapel of Pulcred," are no longer intelligible or if they are, as, surely, in the case of (Car) Radoke's Pool, then we have no indication of whereabouts in the district they may have been.

Robert of Haia's grand-daughter Cecilia married Roger, son of William de Berkerolles and she brought to him the manor of Bassaleg. Roger confirmed his Father and Father-in-law, and grandfather-in law's gifts.

" Know ye, etc., that I, Roger, with the consent of my wife Cecilia, my sons Robert and William, confirm the grant of the lands which my father, William, once gave to Glastonbury and to the church of St. Beselius of Basselech, that is to say the land which begins at the head of Basselech Bridge and from there lies directly up to Lamecosyn. Then it goes through Falesia to the Fountain of Dens and from the Fountain to the road which leads to. . . . . which I gave when my chapel was dedicated. Also, I give and confirm to them the land which begins at Merestoch and runs up to Blanyfoort Eirin. Thence down the river bank to Kemel. Thence near Kemel until it reaches the road which borders my land and so back to Merestoch, For the good of my soul and that of my wife, also for those of my mother, my father and my ancestors I give it together with 20/- for the Service they will do me in my last hours—in other words the Masses that they will say for the repose of my soul." Then came the usual passage about the freedom from feudal payment and burdens. Lastly, the witnesses including, inter alios, Helia the Dean of Basselech, Kudnor of Risca, and Bledri, the third son of Cadifor Fawr.

The de Berkerolles were among the proudest families of Norman Glamorgan. They settled in South Wales about 1146 and held East Orchard and St. Athan. It was about then that Roger acquired Bassaleg through his wife and obtained other lands on the east bank of the Rhymni river.

The Monks at Bassaleg had yet more gifts from their generous and noble patrons, for in 1214-16 we find " Know Ye, that I Isabella, Countess of Gloucester with the consent of my Lord, Geoffrey of Maunderville, confirm my grant to God and the Abbey of Holy Mary and to the Holy Church and Monks of Beisilii juxta Ebod, for the soul of John Travail who died in our service, of the three acres of land which were held by John Hayerlewin. Among the witnesses to this were Henry, Earl of Hereford, Morgan of Caerleon (who held the land under Isabella) and William de Berkerolles (the son of Roger, the son of William).

This Isabella is more often known as Hadwisa or Avice. Her first husband was John, later King of England, who married her in 1176 when he was still a child. He dispensed with her about the time that he came to the throne by obtaining fraudulently the consent of the Pope, and he then married Isabella of Angouleme. Hadwisa proceeded to marry Geoffrey of Mandeville, Earl of Essex, son of Geoffrey FitzPeter, Chief Justiciar of England. When he died she again married, this time the great Hubert de Burgh. As she had no children the estates, which she had obtained from her father, William of Gloucester, passed eventually to her younger sister Amicia, the wife of Richard de Clare. It was during the period of her second marriage that Isabella made this grant to the Monks of Bassaleg.

It was not only the Normans who were good to the Benedictines. The old native aristocracy was equally anxious to assure itself of salvation. " I, Hoel, son of Jonorth, son of Oenus,* with the permission of my Father, for the benefit of the souls of myself, and the souls of all my kinsmen and forbears, also for the commuting of the tithes of Emsanternon† where the White Monks live, do grant, with the object of increasing the substance of the monks living at Bassaleg, 13 acres of land in the marsh of Meinbrit which was formerly held by Kinithuin Glas. ALSO I confirm the grant of a further 12 acres which Morgan, my paternal Uncle, gave unto the said Abbey. ALSO I make a gift of land in the mountains of which these are the boundaries—along the public road which comes from Riworus and goes to the church of Memt Eslim ; the upper part of the boundary is Shrudhlan, that is the river of the church, and the lower boundary is two streams descending on both sides into the aforementioned river." He also granted them the right to graze over all his land and to pasture their swine and hogs in his grove.‡

Memt Eslim is clearly Mynyddislwyn, Shrudhlan is probably the Sirhowy ; and it seems not impossible that " Riworus " is a corruption of whatever was the original of that problematical name " Risca." We shall never

---

* This is Sir Hywel ap Iorweth ap Owain of Caerleon (*see* Chap. XI).

† Emsanternon—Llantarnam.

‡ The full text of all these grants is in Thos. Hearne's " Appendix to Adam of Domerham." Reference can also be made to Dugdale's " Monasticon Anglicarum and Tanner's " Notitia Monastica."

know the exact size of these grants of land, but this was clearly no inconsiderable Priory.

Now the most interesting question is that of the location of the monastic buildings and unfortunately it is just the one we cannot answer. Let Coxe speak again. " No remains of the ancient Priory exist at Bassaleg ; there is however a ruined building at a distance of about a mile in the midst of a deep sequestered Forest not far from the Rumney, not far from the confines of Machen Parish, which is supposed by some to have been part of the Monastery. The name of this Forest, still called Coed y Monachty, seems to confirm the opinion."

I presume it is on the strength of this that the six inch Ordnance Map confidently marks " Site of Priory " at a spot half way down the Machen side of the brook in the middle of Park Wood.

There is undoubtedly a ruin there ; within living memory some of the foundations were knee high. Now one will probably walk over the site a dozen times and not notice the cut stone wall bases scarcely showing above the earth. Short of thorough excavation we shall never know any more about this building.

Was it the Priory ? It seems very doubtful. The building could have been a single cell of earlier or later date ; the wood could have been called Coed y Monachty, simply because it belonged to the monks ; the whole thing may have been invented at a much later date by some person who found the old ruins hidden in the wood and decided that they had once been the Priory. Even as a form of mortification of the flesh it is very difficult to see how worship could have been carried on satisfactorily in church on the banks of the Ebbw by monks who dwelt two and a half miles away on the banks of the Rhymni ! In fact it is an impossible supposition. The Priory must have been close beside whatever building then served as a church. Owing to the early dissolution of the House there has been ample time for all trace of foundations to disappear.

We may say that the Priory was somewhere near the present church site and that short of complete excavation it is impossible to reach any conclusion about the building in Park Wood.

Of the doings of the Benedictine monks of Bassaleg we are fortunate enough to possess a little evidence.

For example there was an agreement and final concord in the name of the Holy and Indivisible Trinity between the Cistercians of Caerleon and the Prior and Monks of Bassaleg made in the presence of the venerable Abbot of Caerleon with the wish, authority and consent of the Prior and Community of Glastonbury. They agreed to submit to the Abbot and Community of Caerleon all quarrels and disputes which had arisen for them to hold until the day when final agreement should be reached, and that then they should be abandoned altogether. But if in the Bassaleg parishes the Monks and Abbot of Caerleon acquired and cultivated any other land then tithes had to be paid or amicably compounded. When final concord was reached the Caerleon Monks gave to Bassaleg ten Marks and four fat beeves as a peace offering. This came between 1101 and 1104, Herwald, Bishop of Llandaff (1056-1104), being one of the witnesses.

In 1190-91 when Henry of Sully was Abbot of Glastonbury—he was appointed by Richard the Lion Heart about 1189 and became Bishop of Worcester in 1193—a document was issued from the Abbey making Roger of Novo Burgo Perpetual Vicar of Bassaleg. At the same time a confirmation of this appointment was issued from Llandaff under the authority of Bishop William Saltmarsh, Prior of Saint Augustine's at Bristol who held the See of Llandaff from 1185 to 1191.

Roger of Novo Burgo—which is apparently Newport—

was by these similar documents granted one mark of
silver a year for life, food as for a monk, horse and a
servant ; also he was to receive the proceeds of the
offertory at his Masses as pocket money—provided that
he said them himself, a half of the proceeds of all deaths
in the parish, and such of the tithes of the monks demesne
as were not accustomed to be taken by the Prior of St.
Augustine's at Bristol.   Roger of Novo Burgo, for his
part, swore that he would not ask the monks for any
further emolument.   Upon his death his office was to
revert to the monks at Bassaleg and they promised not
to make further appointment to any man until the
Abbot of Glastonbury had approved their choice.

Unfortunately for the ecclesiastical fame of Bassaleg,
in 1216 the Priory was broken up by Abbot Michael ;
the monks were recalled to Glastonbury and the land of
Bassaleg with its seven churches was farmed out to the
See of Llandaff at an annual rent of thirty-five marks.
Glastonbury Abbey kept its accounts in a curious fashion.
Instead of pooling all the revenue and drawing sums
therefrom as required, specific portions of each item of
revenue were apportioned to the various objects requiring
disbursement.   Of the thirty-five marks that were to be
received each year from Llandaff it was laid down that
twenty-six were to go to the Abbey cook, four to the
Monk's Hospital, and five to the porter.   This agreement
was recorded both at Glastonbury and Llandaff.

At a later date The Book of Llandaff records revenues
to the Bishop from temporalities pertaining to the church
at Bassaleg of a tithe amounting to £11 0s. 0½d.   These
tithes were to go to the use of " our Lord the Pope or
our Lord the King of England."   The total diocesan
revenue from this source was six marks.

For administrative charges there was annually debited
to the Lord Bishop in the Deanery of Llandaff concerning
the Church at Bassaleg—13s. 4d.

The Annual Debit to pay the Synodal Dues was made
in the Deanery at Newport (Novo Burgo).   Two thirds
went to the Lord Bishop and one third to the Archdeacon.
The debit for Bassaleg was 3s.

Thus we leave the church of Bassaleg till the 16th
century, owned by Glastonbury but leased to the
Bishops of Llandaff.

Some 1300 years after a defensive Iron Age Ring work
was built between Rhiwderin and the Ebbw, another
strongpoint was constructed.   This time it was just the
other side of the river but it protected the same ford of
the river and covered the same stretch of country.   It
was built by Roger of Haia, son of Robert who gave
the land of Bassaleg to God.   Roger of Haia's daughter
Cecilia married Roger, son of William de Berkerolles ;
she brought to him Bassaleg and the new stronghold on
the other side of the Garth Hill.   They called it
Rogerstone after de Haia or de Berkerolles.

In a few years it came by descent to Cecilia's son
William.   William the younger died without issue and
was succeeded by his sister Wenllian, who married into
another great Norman family, Stradling of St. Donats ;
and thus did Rogerstone pass to Sir Edward Stradling.
The strange thing was that the Welsh never called it
Rogerstone.   They preferred to name it after William
de Berkerolles and Tre Gwilym it has remained to this
day, as is exemplified in the name of the main road
through the village.

So Bassaleg passed the 13th century in peace and
obscurity and in 1295 when the Inquisitio Post Mortem
was held on the estates of Gilbert de Clare, Earl of
Gloucester and Hertford, there was recorded :—

> Bassaleg, one fee.
> Ebboth, one fee.
> Deffren Ebboth

and in 1314 when another survey was taken, following

the death of the last De Clare at the battle of Bannockburn, Bassaleg was still " one fee."

After 1314 the overlordship of Glamorgan passed to the Despencers and the Lordship of Wentllwg with it; but when in 1326 the evil day of those men was ended, " Gwynllwg " with Newport, Machen and the Manor Deffren Ebboth reverted to their proper overlords, Margaret de Clare and her husband Hugh of Audley.

On October 30th, 1326, King Edward II, sheltering in South Wales under the wing of the Despencers from the pursuing fury of his wife and the barons, issued a commission to the Cantrefs and Commotes of the Welsh. Among those places which he implored aid were " Maghay " and " Wenthelok," with their Captains Howel ap Iorwerth ap Gruffydd, and Howel ap Dafydd. Alas for King Edward. The men of Wentllwg with all the Welsh of the mountains of Morganwg had no cause to love the Norman overlords when they were men such as the Despencers. Their refusal to raise a finger to help him led directly to his capture above the Rhondda and to the dreadful, sinister screams proceeding from the dungeon of Berkeley Castle which marked the wretched monarch's end.

Peace descended once again on South Wales and for Bassaleg it meant the most glorious period of a long history.

CHAPTER VI.

GREAT MEN AT GWERN Y CLEPPA.

LLEWELYN ap Ifor ap Llewelyn Lleia ap Ifor ap Llewelyn ap Ifor ap Bleddri ap Cadifor Fawr was of high birth. Had it been three hundred years earlier he might have been Prince of the West. As it was he was Lord of St. Clears in Dyfed.

Syr Morgan ap Meredydd ap Gruffydd ap Meredydd* was of the old royal house of Gwent, was lord of Machen, and lived at Tref Ddegr (Tredegar). He died in 1331, not before, so popular story has it, his men had learnt to sing the greatest battle song of the Monmouthshire border, that immortal and most stirring of marching songs " Rhyfelgyrch Capten Morgan " (the war march of Captain Morgan).†

Angharad, his daughter, married the great man from Dyfed. They had three sons. Morgan, the eldest, came to Tredegar; the second was Ifor of Gwern y Cleppa in Bassaleg and Philip, the youngest, was of Machen.

It is Ifor, who concerns us. He was nicknamed Ifor Hael, Ifor the Generous, married Nest, daughter of Rhys ap Grono ap Llewarch, and his sole claim to fame was that he had as a relative Dafydd ap Gwilym, the greatest of all Welsh Poets.

Of Dafydd's life little is certain save what can be found in his poems but a truly amazing supply of doubtful tradition has contrived to make up the deficiency.

---

* For who ancestry see under Machen in Chaper XI.
† Which should never be confused with " Dewch i'r Frwydr " (Forth to the Battle).

He must have been born at least as early as 1339 ; for one thing, he wrote a poem to Hywel ap Tewdwr who was Dean of Bangor from 1359 to 1370 and furthermore, he must have been quite 25 and probably 30 when his patron died in 1361. In another poem he wishes the " Bwa Bach," the Little Hunchback, the husband of his love, would go to the French War with Rhys Gwrgan. The last of Edward III's French Wars was in 1369. Dafydd makes no mention of Owain Glyndwr and Iolo Goch, another great poet of the period, probably went to the Court of Owain (1400) after writing of the death of Dafydd.

So Dafydd probably lived somewhere between 1330 and 1400. His father was Gwilym Gam, his mother Ardudful Fychan, sister of Llewelyn ap Gwilym Fychan of Emlyn, Lord of Ceredigion. These people were kinsfolk of Ifor Hael. Dafydd's birthplace was probably Llanbadarn Fawr, although Iolo Morganwg, for no good reason, puts it in a ditch at Llandaff. Equally uncertain tales educate him in Italy and return him later to Ifor, when he probably became steward or held some similar household post, because he continued to enjoy the hospitality of Gwern y Cleppa until Ifor and Nest died. His reputation as a lover has always been great and he is supposed to have indulged in what has been called the " supreme mental abandonment " of wooing twenty-four maidens at the same time ! There is still a tale in Bassaleg of how he would sit on Cwrt y Defaid Hill and sing to the local lasses in the sunset. This, when coupled with his appearance, makes a delightful picture. The Reverend D. Jones, Llanfair, recorded in 1572 " I have talked with a very old woman who had seen another who had talked with Dafydd ap Gwilym and she said he was very tall and slender with yellow hair flowing in ringlets, and it was full of silver clasps and rings." Of Ifor's daughter it was said—and there could be no lovelier description—that her hair was " as the colour of fire at the Battle of Camlan."

To leave the borderline of legend and come back to facts, the first thirteen poems in the 1789 edition were concerned with this part of Dafydd's life. Much scholarship is required before his real work can be sifted from the spurious additions but of the thirteen, Professor Williams regards the first six and the last one as genuine. It is fortunate that among these are the only specific references to Bassaleg.

From No. 2 A Cherddi Cildannau'n deg
            A Solos Ym Massaleg.

" The poetry, song and beautiful harp music of Bassaleg."

From 4 Arglwyddiaeth dugiaeth deg
       A Seiliwyd Ym Massaleg.

"A Lordship, a fair dukedom was founded in Bassaleg"

From 4 Nid oes bren yn y Wenallt
       Na bo'n wyrdd ei ben a'i wallt.

" There's not a tree on the Wenallt the hair of whose head is not green."

Dafydd wrote much in praise of his munificent patron. For example, " I ddiolch am Fenyg Ifor Hael " thanks him for a pair of gloves, the one containing gold, the other silver. Unfortunately, Professor Williams regards as spurious the fine cywyddau on the countryside of Morganwg found in the appendix. Alas, death comes all too soon to this happy period of Dafydd's life. Poem number thirteen is the " Marwnad Ifor Hael a Nest ei Wraig."

It would appear, or Iolo Morganwg made it appear, that in the summer of 1361 the lord of Gwern y Cleppa and his wife paid a visit to John Pascal, Bishop of Llandaff, at his palace of Llangadwaladr beyond Newport now called Bishton. There is mention in the poem of " Godechaint " and " Trymhaint,"—lurking and deadly pestilence. 1361 was a bad plague year and plague at that time could be as frequent as the common cold to-day. One never recovered ; it spared none, not even the Queen's Majesty,* let alone a Lord of Wentlooge, his beloved wife, and My Lord the Bishop of Llandaff.

Dafydd is then lost to us. We have nothing further from him upon the corner of Wales he loved so much. He must have left it for his native Dyfed, and there met with the one who was to be his Beatrice and his Laura, Morfudd the beautiful, daughter of Madog Lawgain of Mon. (Anglesey). To her he wrote 147 poems.

Dafydd's poetry was primarily a poetry of nature. Unlike the contemporary French verse it uses love, not as an all-consuming theme, but as a temple in which to display his marvellous worship of the beauties of the countryside. His was the simple love of nature of W. H. Davies rather than the mystical inward eye of Wordsworth. " In his class he yields not a palm to any other. Dafydd is the most distinguished of all Welsh poets. If it were not impossible to translate his cywyddau he would rank among the greatest of all mediæval poets." If ! Much of the beauty of Welsh poetry lies in its metre. The Cywydd is made of seven-syllable lines rhyming in couplets and it is impossible to render more than the bare sense into English ; the intricacies of rhyme, rhythm and alliteration are beyond all translation. Dafydd, 'Dafydd gywydd Gwin' Dafydd of the wine sweet cywydd, is only for those lucky enough to possess the speech of their fathers ; but there are those who say that it is worth the trouble of learning Welsh to enter that world of his.

It is impossible to leave ap Gwilym without dealing with the supposed " Eisteddfod of Gwern y Cleppa."

The Iolo MSS. contain a mass of stuff relating to ap Gwilym ; it repeats most of the popular tradition as

---

* Anne of Bohemia, d. 1394, wife of Richard II.

solemn fact and gives wholly unsupported accounts of
many incidents in his life. For example, the story of
the poet's burial at Strata Florida is discounted even by
Taliesin Williams who edited his father's manuscripts.

Iolo Morganwg's real name was Edward Williams
(1747-1826). He did not scruple to invent " history "
or to distort truth if he thought that thereby he could
glorify his homeland and it is he who popularised and
perhaps originated the story of the three Eisteddfods.
The first, he says, was at Gwern y Cleppa. The Cywydd
was raised to fame as the leading Chair metre and Dafydd
by his sheer genius was made Chief Bard of Glamorgan
as " Dafydd Morganwg." The second Eisteddfod was
at Dol Goch in Emlyn and was attended by Sion of
Kentchurch and Rhys Goch Eryri. The third was at
Maelor in Powys under Earl Mortimer and Iolo Goch
was present. The Iolo MSS. put Dafydd's dates as
earlier than we would now allow, 1300-1368, but this
would have fitted quite well, although he shows no sign
of age in 1361 when Ifor died ; there is, however, a slip.
Rhys Goch Eryri was not born till 1365 and probably
lived till about 1440, while Sion Cent died about 1400.
Nowadays the Eisteddfod story is generally regarded as a
fabrication. For once quoting his source Iolo Morganwg
says he took it from " Notices of the Bards and Poets
from the MSS. of Edward Dafydd of Margam " by
Anthony Powell. This sounds vague enough.

However, we are not all critical scholars of those
makers of mere romance out of so much that had once the
magic of mystical historic truth. Let us pursue the
matter no further and keep our Eisteddfodau. There
is so little glory in Bassaleg that it is worth fighting hard
for every scrap we have.

What of Gwern y Cleppa itself ? To Coxe and
Barber at the turn of the Nineteenth Century the house
was already nothing more than a pile of ruin hidden in

thickets.   In the mid-twentieth it is a mass of foundations barely rising through grass, weed and bramble.   It lies to the right of the path which goes down the hedge on the Newport side of Gwern y Cleppa Wood.   Cross over the main ride where it leaves the path and after a few paces go ten yards into the wood to the right.   That is the middle of the site of the once great Court of Ifor Hael.

Although it was probably still occupied in 1632, when Roger Morgan of Gwern y Cleppa was buried at Bassaleg, I suspect that the house lay in ruins many years before the land was finally passed over to Tredegar. In 1789 we were told it had been desolate for at least a century and the Reverend Evan Evans had by then said of it :—

> " Y Llwybrau gynt lle bu'r gam
>   Yw Lleoedd y Dylluan "

rendered very freely

" The paths formerly devoted to song are now the haunts of the owl."

In 1570 Saxton, the map maker, marked it, not as a park like Tredegar, but as a village distinct from Bassaleg. He was of course followed by the other London map makers who continued to copy his place names right down to the eighteenth century.   So we find Gwern y Cleppa still marked as a village some time after the house had ceased to be inhabited.

It was only by measuring and marking, clearing and digging, that anything could be done with the site at all but a day's work at the most revealed that at one it had been a very large house.   The Westward frontage of the buildings was at least 240 feet long, the Eastward about 300 feet.   A walled enclosure lay to the South and was 70 feet by 75, from one outer thickness of the 5 foot walls to the other.   While this seems too large to be a Great Hall of the period, it could perhaps have been a walled or semi-fortified courtyard.

The main structure appears to have been quite 100 feet wide at the greatest extent but in the confused mass of rock and earth it is hard to tell foundation from mere collapsed stonework and piles of rubble.

We need not grieve overmuch. Gwern y Cleppa may be dead but Dafydd ap Gwilym will be with us for ever.

CHAPTER VII.

A SQUIREARCHY, ITS CHURCHES AND ITS QUARRELS.

A T the close of the middle ages the social and commercial structure in Wales underwent changes very similar to those which occurred in England. Between the 14th and 17th centuries the revolution, though gradual, is decisive. Overlords become squires, serfs become hired labourers, civic corporations and wealthy burghers come into their own ; in addition, although we hear little about them there probably develops a class of freeholding yeomen farmers which lasted about 250 years. Norman families disappear ; the great names of Morgan, Herbert, and Kemeys, come to the fore to an even greater extent until by 1700 they hold a high proportion of the Manors of Monmouthshire. Towards the end of this period the yeomen freeholder paying his dues to a semi-feudal Manor becomes a tenant farmer paying his rent to the Great House and its estate.

A proper measure of Law and Order followed the development of the Justices of the Peace and the breaking down of the power of the Barons. The Council of Wales and the Marches was set up and by Statute of 1536, the old Lordships of Gwent became the Shire of Monmouth. The cantref of Wentllwg was rent from Morganwg, to which it has always belonged in spirit, and made a part of the new County where Welsh custom was no longer to run and the Lord King's Commission of the Peace would ensure to each man security of life, limb and property.

The last development was that of the labourer's cottage. Not till the very late seventeenth century did these feature prominently in our country scene.

During this period, when the countryside slowly took on its modern appearance and organisation, there were some entertaining people in and around Bassaleg. They lived a comparatively peaceful life. Owain Glyndwr swept through ravaging and burning in 1400, but the Wars of the Roses hardly came at all and the Great Civil War though exciting enough, with fighting at Raglan, Chepstow or St. Fagans and with Cromwell marching through to the West, had little local incident.

To deal first with Gwern y Cleppa—Ifor Hael had a son Thomas, who had a son Morgan who was married in 1410. His son John Hir was Coroner of Wentlooge 1447-48. Morgan John married in 1487 Nest, daughter of Jevan Gwyn ap Gwilym David of Rhiwperra and had issue William Morgan and grandson Philip Morgan (1517-81). Philip married Ann, daughter of Rowland Morgan of Machen and of his issue Roger Morgan, second son, was of Gwern y Cleppa and was buried at Bassaleg in July, 1632, at the age of 76. Philip's eldest son, Henry married in 1571 or 1581. Henry's son Rowland was living anyway between 1604 and 1628 and he had 1 Edmund, 2 Thomas, 3 Edward, 4 Rowland of Craig y Saeson, who died in 1693. Edmund Morgan married in 1621, his son Colonel Myles Morgan was dead by 1678; Myles had a son Rowland who had a son Myles who sold Gwern y Cleppa to John Morgan of Tredegar on the 13th of October, 1733.

Thus the long line of Morgan of Gwern y Cleppa came to an end. Its house had been pulled down or had fallen into complete ruin years before.

Rogerstone Castle passed through the descendants of Wenllian and Sir Edward Stradling until in the 15th Century Sir Henry Stradling of St. Donats was foolish enough to get taken by a Breton pirate called Colyn Dolphin, a Celt of Armorica, off his native Brittany coast. Sir Henry's ransom was 2000 marks and to raise it the Stradlings had to sell Sutton in Glamorgan and Rogerstone with Tregwillim in Wentllwg. As an indication of date, Sir Henry's son Thomas died under 26 years of age in September 1480.

The Kemeys family bought Rogerstone. In 1439 John Kemeys 3rd son of John ap Jevan was Lord of Rogerstone and his son William was Constable of Newport Castle, 10th December 1446, Mayor of Newport in 1447 and Lord of Rogerstone and Sutton 1470-85. He also had Sir Harry Stradling's town house on the site of the Westgate. Roger Kemeys, who was under age in 1595, sold Rogerstone in 1611 and Sutton in 1614. Thus the Kemeys family acquired some form of tenancy in the Manor of Rogerstone and lost it. The present Castle House, a building of the late 17th century, has no connection with these people.

However, about 1520 a daughter of Sir Thomas Gamage of Coyty married a Richard Grant of Rogerstone so that although no houses of any great age exist there at the present day, Rogerstone was not only a castle.

There was not only a family of Morgan of Gwern y Cleppa but also a Morgan of Bassaleg. One of the great great grandsons of Llewelyn ap Ifor was Sir John Morgan of Tredegar and Sir John's second son Thomas was of Machen Plas. Of Thomas we shall hear more in Chapter XI ; it was his third son, John, alive in 1568, who founded the branch of Morgan of Bassaleg. John of Bassaleg had four sons :—1 Rowland of Bassaleg, who in his turn had two, a Rowland of St. Brides and another Thomas, 2 William, whose widow married a David Roberts of Bassaleg, 3 Henry, officer of the customs at Cardiff, 4 Thomas, known as " Thomas Morgan the

Conspirator," born in 1543. He became Secretary to the Protestant Bishop of Exeter and then, in 1569, to Lord Shrewsbury at Tutbury where Mary, the Queen of Scots, was being held a prisoner by Elizabeth of England. He became a devoted follower of the romantic and unhappy Queen and after imprisonment for complicity in the Ridolfi plot of 1571 fled to Paris. Later when the Jesuit Parry was hanged for plotting to kill Queen Elizabeth he accused Thomas of having abetted him and Thomas was imprisoned in France. He remained in constant secret communication with Mary until her execution and in him she placed the utmost trust, appointing him to act as her sole confidential agent at Rome. Released at Paris he went to Flanders only to be taken by the Duke of Parma and forced to undergo examination by the Spanish Inquisition. The Inquisitors were displeased to find that he was against subjecting England to Roman Catholicism by the use of Foreign troops " and especially Spaniards " and that, because he thought the work could be done from the inside, he was creating a division of opinion among English Catholics. Luckily, the Duke of Parma died so Thomas was once more released and was living at Rome until 1595 with Doctor Owen Lewis, the Bishop of Casano. In 1596 he went to France again but was promptly ejected and did not return to that country till 1605. Although Guy Fawkes, in his confession, said that Thomas had mooted a gunpowder plot against Elizabeth he had not taken part in the famous conspiracy of November 1605, possibly because James the First and Sixth was the son of his Mary of Scotland to whose memory he remained ever faithful. Thomas was still alive as late as January 1611.

There is no house in Bassaleg that dates back to the

mid-sixteenth century so we have no indication of where these Morgans may have lived.*

It has been said that the Welsh squires " did not observe the sacrament of matrimony too closely." John of Bassaleg had a natural son Thomas born out of wedlock who was living at Bettws in 1587. Thus was founded from Morgan of Bassaleg a bastard branch which lived a life of sturdy mediocrity till 1812. It included George Morgan, an attorney at law at Newport, who was steward of the Manor of Rogerstone from 1639 to 1654. His son Henry was an Alderman of Newport in 1714 and lies in St. Woolos and after three more Georges the line faded away when Charles, brother of the last George, died on July 25th, 1812.

The eldest son of Thomas of Machen Plas was another Rowland Morgan. Rowland's second son Henry and Henry's son Thomas were of Llanrhymney. Thomas of Llanrhymney's third son Robert was living in London in 1670. It was Robert's son Henry who became notorious as Sir Henry Morgan the Buccaneer. He was born about 1635 and died in 1684 being Governor of Jamaica 1675-80 and spending most of his life in the West Indies. He was thus of a very minor branch of the Morgan family and, contrary to popular belief, had nothing whatsoever to do with this district.

The senior great grandson of Thomas of Machen was William of Tredegar, Knighted in 1637. His son was Rowland of Risca and Rowland's son Colonel William Morgan was buried at Bassaleg church on the 27th October, 1679.

---

* The above account of Thomas the Conspirator is taken from the Translations of the Hon. Society of Cymrodorion 1901-2, pps. 124-127. Reference can be made to sources, which are there set out in full, and also to the invaluable " Limbus Patrum " of Mr. George Thomas Clark of Talygarn. Although it is not always accurate, this book still offers the most conveniently accessible and comprehensive aid to anyone wishing to straighten out the tangled threads of these Morgan pedigrees.

At this time there were few persons of standing in the neighbourhood who were not in some way connected with the main family. It was indeed Morgan country. Even the Hopkins of Machen had a common origin with Tredegar. Thomas ap Syr David ap Phillip, youngest brother of Ifor Hael, was father of John living in 1490. John was father of Hopkin Bedel, alive at Machen in 1523 ; Hopkin had issue, 1 Thomas Hopkin, Mayor of Newport 1519-23, 2 Roger Hopkins and 3 John Hopkins, Bailiff of Bassaleg. The line survived through two Georges and an Edward, vanishing about 1650.

This abundant class of people, members of the great and growing county gentry if they were lucky enough to be born the eldest sons, were mere yeomen if they were of cadet or collateral branches. They were baptized, wed, and buried at the churches of Bassaleg and Machen whose present buildings must have been constructed not more than a century before the opening of this period.

What happened to the Administration of Bassaleg Church is clear. Shortly before the Dissolution when Glastonbury was visited by Henry VIII's Commissioners enquiring into the state of the Monasteries we find this account :—" TEMPORALITIES IN WALES. The Manor of Barslake. The Rentes of Assize apperteynynge unto the said Manor of Barslake always payable at the Feast of thannunciacion of our Ladye and Saincte Michaell Tharcangell, as it dothe appere in olde terrore (*sic*. terrier) are of the yearly value of Vis,Viii d. The site of the said Manor with the demaynes apperteynynge thereto are letten out by indenture divers yeres Unto the Kynges Most High Majesty as it dothe appere in the books of Accoumptes to the Some of xxiii l."

" Some total of Temporalities in Wales xxiiil Vis Viiid."

This document shows that the annual value of the

Manor was no light sum—several hundred pounds in present day value. The Manor was in fact " Letten out diverse years," three hundred years to be correct, to the Lord Bishop of Llandaff but either it had been sublet to the King or else in those days of temporal assertiveness it was wiser to say that Ecclesiastical Manors belonged to the Crown. The Commissioners at Glastonbury were not the pleasantest of people.*

At the dissolution of the Monasteries the Manor of Bassaleg lost its four hundred year old attachment to Glastonbury and went completely to Llandaff for nearly two centuries.

On 15th October 1586 the Chapter of Llandaff confirmed a grant made by the Bishop to Queen Elizabeth of the Manor and Lordship of Bassaleg. The grant was evidently for a term of years only, as on 10th September 1660 the Chapter confirmed a lease by the Bishop for twenty years of the Manor and Lordship of Bassaleg with seven churches. The Mother Church of Wentllwg still had her flock around her.

The Squires were good to their Churches. In 1578 Miles Morgan of Tredegar (No longer spelt Tref Ddegr Ymassalec) made his will and in it he made provision for grants :—

" Towards the building of the Steeple (?) of the parish church of Bassaleg £6 13s. 4d. Towards the relief of the poor people of the said parish of Bassaleg £3 6s. 8d. To my wyfe Katherine, My sayde wyfe, towards the Mayntenance of her house during her abode and continuance at Tredegar all that part and portion of the tithe corn and grain within the Parish of Bassaleg and now in the tenure and occupation of My Lord Bishop of Llandaf."

---

* At this time the King was holding the lordship of Wentllwg direct.

In 1674 the will of William Morgan of Tredegar made a bequest " to the poor of the parishes of Machen, Bassaleg and the town of Newport £200, to be set out to the best advantage of the said poor." In 1698 he was followed by Charles Morgan. " I give and bequeath to the poor of Bassaleg in the County of Monmouth the sum of £20 of the good and lawful money of England."

The generosity of the local aristocracy was not only testamentary. It is recorded on a board in Bassaleg Church that in 1670 Madam Kate Morgan gave £5 per annum to the poor and that in 1675 Rowland Morgan gave by annual rentcharge on Tredegar a further £14 per annum together with £20 per annum to provide the parish with a schoolmaster. At the same time Mr. John Morgan also gave 50s. per annum to the poor.

The English structure of squirearchy was now complete It was the Squire's wish, pleasure, and duty to see to the well being of the parish poor.

I have said that life went on in comparative peace ; but did it ? When these people quarrelled they did not do it half-heartedly. There must have been men of Bassaleg and Machen in High Street, Newport, on the fatal Sunday morning of February 23rd, 1533, when, on his way to the Church of St. Woolos, George ap Morgan and his men were attacked by the rival gang of Walter and William Herbert after a picked quarrel over a greyhound. In the ensuing tumult the clergy from St. Woolos are said to have turned out to try and make peace, only to be sent packing up Stow Hill in ignominious flight. "After which divers goodly fellows were hurt and slain and one maiden was seized and taken on horseback, screaming horribly all the time, many miles into the country, and there dreadfully done by and never seen again ! "

It was the business of the Star Chamber to check

such hearty, antisocial disturbances, and the records of many of the lawsuits heard before it would doubtless be as highly entertaining as the one previously published from which I have quoted. Several of these records are concerned with Bassaleg.*

(1) Phillip Edwards of Milton. Complaint against Morgan Owen and wife, Ievan Williams et alios, that they made forcible entry on a disputed devise of the land of William Morgan of Gwern y Cleppa in Coedcernyw.

(2) Ievan Ievan of Bettws versus David Meyrick, Rosser Phillip, et alios. concerning the custom of land-holding in the Manor of Rogerstone.

(3) Lewis James, gent., versus Howell William, William Morgan, et alios. Complaint :—Lying in Wait, violent assaults, and shooting with guns at Bassaleg.

(4) Lancelot Andrewes, Bishop of Ely, versus Thomas Jenkins. Concerning goods and debts of Roland Ievan of Bassaleg, Suicide.

(5) William Jones of Llansantfraed, nephew and executor of William Williams of Newport versus Richard Williams of Newport the brother of William Williams, Thomas Williams, Roger Williams the Shoemaker, John Morgan et alios. Complaint :—forcible ousters at Bassaleg and Newport and seizure of deeds and grain.

(6) Grffiith Morgan of Llantarnam, Yeoman v. Rowland Morgan of Gwern y Cleppa, gent, John Morgan, Andrew and John Thomas, Thomas Lewis, et alios. Complaint :—Assault with pistols at Pont y Maustre on the road to Cardiff.

(7) Thomas William of Panteg, James Jones of Llantilio Crosenny, gent., v. Sir William Morgan of

---

* Full Public Record Office references to these cases can be found in the catalogue of Welsh Star Chamber Records compiled by Mr. Ifan ap Owen Edwards. They are all of the reigns of Elizabeth and James I.

Tredegar, Knight, Howell David of Risca et alios, his servants John Vizard et alios. Complaint :—Assault between Panteg and Bassaleg. Drinking the Complainant's blood mixed with ale (! ! !). Attack on a House.

Here are seven cases five of which are concerned with violence. No. It was not always peaceful.

The reference in case 6 to " Pont y Maustre " is interesting. Although spoken of as being on the road to Cardiff, this place can only be Pont y Mister by Risca. We do not know the meaning or derivation of this curious name and while " Maustre " is nearer the original than " Mister " it still does not give us the answer.

It is clear that at the end of the period covered by this chapter the oldest name in South Wales—Morgan —was rising rapidly. Morgan occupied the land of every former freeholder in the district ; Morgan with its Headquarters at Tredegar and main outpost at Machen, took in not only the land of other families but also of its own collateral branches—Gwern y Cleppa, Bassaleg, Graig y Saeson and the like. Some remained as tenants ; others eventually sank in status and provide the innumerable Morgan families in the populous South Wales of to-day. At the end of the 17th Century a great part of the Hundred of Wentllwg had collected together into one large and efficient organization, the estate of Morgan of Tredegar.

Two 17th Century Houses.

The 18th Century dawns on an agricultural community. There is a big estate with tenant farmers. The organisation is still that of the mediæval manor but it is becoming a technical method of landholding rather than the basis of social existence. Not all the land is yet cultivated, there is more forest, more wilderness, less farms, fewer hedges, stone thatched cottages for the labourers are only just appearing. The villagers still have true rights of common on the manorial waste. The old fallow system is practised, livestock is undersized, root crops unknown. There is the present Tredegar House, very new, much as we see it to-day, Rogerstone Castle House and the church; there is presumably a Vicarage, probably on the site of the present one; there are some cottages, but apparently there was no Church Farm. With two exceptions, no 17th Century buildings survive in Bassaleg to-day. The first exception, Croesheolydd Farm, is a building of about 1620-40 : and what a lovely building it is ! While not pretending to the more recent size and magnificence of Tredegar or the older grandeur of Machen Plas it yet preserves a grace of form and construction that rank it well up in the list of 16th and 17th Century Monmouthshire farmhouses. Invisible from the Michaelstone and Pen y lan roads it is like a jewel in a setting of its own fields and orchards, hidden away in the hollow of the Bassaleg brook.

There is no evidence of an earlier house having existed on the site, or who were builders or tenants of Croesheolydd but it has ornamentation and a spaciousness which proclaim that it was no ordinary tenant farm. It must have been the abode of somebody with pretentions to gentility and certain resources of capital. Perhaps it was a house of some branch of the Morgan family but there is no mention of Morgan of Croesheolydd either in pedigree or on the tombs in the church.

In construction it is, like most old Monmouthshire farm houses, a cross between the stone of the Cotswolds and the half timbering of the Counties further up the Welsh border.

Originally the downstairs structure was based on the usual two room principle. There was a great hall into

CROESHEOLYDD.   M. EDMONDS.

which led the front door and the porch ; opposite to
them led out the great staircase. The great chimney
and fireplace were part of the back wall of this vast
chamber and the back door and lean-to larder were
beside the great chimney. The stairs leading up to the
spacious attics came in the thickness of the wall at the
South Eastern corner. Three-quarters or more of the
way along the building was another massive wall. Beyond
this was a small Parlour and beyond this again the
Western outer wall and second chimney.

About 1840 the West gable fell or became unsafe and
was replaced by the modern brick wall. At the same
time the opportunity was taken to extend the Jacobean
two-chamber ground plan into a modern form by adding
a brick chimney each side of the old massive partition
wall and by putting in several thin partitions—thus
creating out of what had been the great Hall a passage,
kitchen and drawing room. This gave in all three
downstairs rooms. The Great Hall plan of the mediæval
house is rather draughty to modern susceptibilities.

Of the internal fittings the great staircase leading ot
the family bedroom is the most notable. It is no less
than six feet wide. Its posts and blocks are of immense
thickness and the bannisters and newels are very note-
worthy ; the knobs are modern.

In the attic, which presumably served as stores and
servants' bedrooms, the main truss beams have turned,
slotted, mortice and tenon ties, with tie pins to secure.

The date of the house, with the exception of the
obviously late 18th Century lean-to Dairy west of the
great staircase extension, is somewhere in the 1620-40
period. To judge solely by external appearances the
main structure could be as old as 1600 but the ornamentation of the stairs portion tells of a construction, in
England between 1610-20 but here in South Wales not
before 1620-40. It might have been possible that the

stairs were added twenty years after the main building,
but the fact that the ornamentation of the cellar door
hinge-straps below the great staircase is the same as
that on the hinge-straps of the front door, would
indicate that the entire structure is of the one period.

The stone window hoods on the Eastern wall are of
Elizabethan type but they remained in use well into the
Jacobean period.

No history attaches to this house.   There are some
rather gory tales in the village presenting it with battles
and massacres of an impossibly early date.   Croesheolydd
pond, which has no visible inlet or outflow, is packed
with the corpses of the slain ;   Bassaleg brook which,
mark you, never runs dry, reddens with the blood of the
dying ;   armies march to its attack and defence from all
over the place ;   Morgan ap Meredydd can be heard
singing his war march in the distance.   Alas !   It is all
moonshine.   Croesheolydd is a peaceful dwelling house,
not more than three centuries old and from Brynhedydd
in the summer sunset it is very beautiful.

The second survival of seventeenth century Bassaleg
is a house built on an altogether smaller scale than
Croesheolydd.   Although it has no structural detail that
would enable us to assign it to an exact decade this house,
the keeper's house, below Messrs. Whitehead's Recreation
Ground in Tredegar Park, has architectural features not
essentially dissimilar from those of its larger contemporary.   It was clearly the abode of some yeoman farmer
and was later enclosed and reduced in status when
Tredegar made its great deer park.

As we enter the house through the typical period
porch there lies to our right the immense thickness of
the great dividing wall and beyond that the private
parlour.   The great hall, sub-divided in the 18th century
into a small sitting room with kitchens, is to the left
and in its front wall is the great chimney.   Straight

ahead through the modern door is the staircase. This
feature has not the majestic breadth of its superb fellow
at Croesheolydd. After an initial flight it branches
right and left into what prove to be two completely
separate sections of the upper story. In each section
a thin lath wall sub-divides the great bedroom into two,
giving four chambers in all, and in each a staircase leads
up to the capacious roof attic. In the right hand section
the ascent is made above the main staircase, but in that,
to the left, a narrow passage is cut up in the great thickness of the central dividing wall. This ascent is now
blocked by a plaster barrier but can be found to have
emerged in the attic at that point in the central wall
where a doorway is let through giving access from one
side of the loft to the other. Thus on the ground floor
and in the attic there is access from one half to the other,
through the wall, whereas on the first floor it is necessary
to go down and up the branches of the main staircase.

As at Croesheolydd the roof beams are slotted and
morticed with tie pins to secure.

The walls of this house are coated with stone and
cement. We miss the rich warmth of the cream plastering
at Croesheolydd and, no doubt, many constructional
features are covered over. Nevertheless these 17th
century builders had their hearts in their craft. They
built with form and grace. They built to last. Cover
it with what you will their style is both unmistakeable
and lovely.

CHAPTER VIII.

THE LORDSHIP OF WENTLLWG AND ITS MANORS

THE manorial records of Wentllwg are of great interest. The ones that we have are only about two and a half centuries old but, doubtless, they contain the ancient Custom of the Lordship. When these Courts, the records of which we shall examine, were held there were many more tenant farmers than there had been when Croesheolydd was built a century before. There was still more common land and waste but in most respects the countryside had taken on its modern appearance. In theory, the manorial structure prevailed down to 1925 and did not breathe its last till January 1st, 1940, when, for what minute sum they were still worth, the last feudal dues were extinguished. Long before the 20th century the main business went on in the solicitors office and the tenant's duty to do suit of court cost him far less in feudal rent services than it cost the Lord in supper and beer. Here then is the echo of a social organization that was the basis of life throughout the Middle Ages and with Copyhold tenure still in existence was an active force as a means of land transfer, entry, and inspection in the 18th and 19th Centuries. Look well at it : its like will not be seen in Wentllwg again.

The Lordship of Wentllwg was a lordship dependant on Glamorgan which was conquered by Robert FitzHamon. From his daughter, Mabel it passed into the hands of the Earls of Gloucester and Clare. With the exception of a brief period when it was in the hands of the Despencers it remained a de Clare lordship until in 1342 the daughter of Margaret de Clare and Hugh of Audley married Ralph, Earl Stafford. The Staffords lost it when Edward Stafford, Duke of Buckingham, was beheaded in 1521. Then it was held directly by the Kings of England until in 1547 Edward VI granted it to William Herbert, first Earl of Pembroke. The Earls of Pembroke held it until 1710 when it finally passed into Morgan hands.*

The Lordship was held of the King and within it each manor had its own feudal descent. Bassaleg, for example, passed from FitzHamon to Robert of Haia who in turn granted it to the Church. Although often leased out to the Crown it remained in Ecclesiastical hands until the late years of the Seventeenth Century when it was acquired first by the Beauforts and then by the Morgans. Rogerstone, as we have seen in Chapter VII, descended from Robert of Haia through the Stradlings and was bought and sold by the Kemeys. In 1700 we find it held by Edmund Morgan of Penllwyn Sarph and Bedwellty since when it has come into the Herbert family.

On the 16th day of September, 1700, the twelfth year of the reign of King William III, a Jury of Survey presented its findings to the trustees of Thomas, Earl of Pembroke and Montgomery, Lord of the Lordship of Wentlooge. Their commission was to survey all Honors, Manors, Lands, and Tenements, Forests, Chases, Parks and Wastes in the said Lordship. They reported that they found the said Lordship to lie in the parishes of " Bassaleg, Rumney, Peterstone, St. Mellence, St. Brides, Marchfield, Michellston y Vedow, Coedcernew,

---

* Since writing it there has come to the author's notice a most full and scholarly account contained in certain papers read to the Cambrian Archæological Association at Newport, in 1885, and published by the Monmouthshire and Caerleon Antiquarian Associatiou (1886).

St. Woolloos, Bettus, Malpas, Llanvihangel-Llantarnam and Risk(a)." Its boundaries were the rivers " Uske Seaverne and Rumney and the lordships of Machen and Porth Mawre."

It comprised the following manors :—

Rumney.	In the tenure of Phillip Herbert.
Hensham.	In the tenure of Thomas Morgan of Llanrumney.
Greenfield.	
Redcastle.	
Sutton.	In the tenure of Thomas Morgan of Tredegar.
Fitzjohn De la Moore.	
Youlton.	
Peterston.	
Diffrin.	
Cogan Fleming.	
Cogan Pembroke.	
Bassaleg.	In the tenure of the Dowager Duchess of Beaufort.*
Malpas.	
Mendalgiffe.	In the tenure of the Lord of the Lordship and with a separate survey done by their own tenants.
English and Welsh Dowle.	
Pencarn.	
Hencourt.	In the tenure of Sir John Thomas of Wenvo.
St. Brides.	
Rogerstone.	In the tenure of Edmund Morgan of Penllwyn Sarph.

The jury presented that in all the manors of Wentllwg except Bassaleg, Rumney, Hensham, Peterstone and Greenfield or Ebboth, which had their own custom,

---

* Wife of Henry, 1st Duke of Beaufort, (died 1699). Succeeded by his Grandson, Henry (died 1714):

all tenants had to attend the May and Michaelmas
Courts Leet under penalty of a forty shilling fine if they
were not present.   Tenants also owed suit at the monthly
Courts Baron and, in order that everyone might know
who were the tenants, a feudal rent roll of all the manors
was appended to the survey.   Upon the death of the
Lord the tenants had to pay to the manor a heriot of
the best quick beast which they had on their land.   If
there was no such beast then a payment of 5s. had to
be made "in the name of a Heriot."   We may safely take
it that at this late date the payment of a head of one's
best cattle—an intolerable mediæval burden—was no
longer made, and that the 5s., worth but a fraction of
its ancient value, had taken its place. Sometimes it is just
called " a Heriot of 5s."   Having assured the Lord that
they knew of no customary rights or services other than
those mentioned, the Presenters went on to say that the
only royalties due to the Lord were " Waifes, Estrayes,
Felons Goods, Treasure trove, Deodands, Escheats, and
Muniments like Profits if any should happen."   They
said that there were two Pounds or Pinfolds in the
Lordship for the impounding of straying beasts.   One of
these was at Stow in the parish of St. Wooloos but the
efforts made at describing the whereabouts of the other
are little more use to us to-day than were the boundaries
of the lands given in the monastic grants.   Place names
change more often than is generally supposed.   The
right to keep the Lord's pound and to collect the fees
paid by those who came to reclaim their animals was
let out at a rent.   At every May leet the Grand Jury
appointed a tenant to serve by ancient custom as Coroner
or Reeve and it was his duty to collect all the rents and
fines in the coming year.   The Coroner, Reeve, or
Bailiff could appoint a deputy but remained responsible
for the consequences of any loss caused to the tenants
through his deputy's neglect.   In the Eighth article it

was declared that if the Lord died a payment was rated on the tenants of each manor of £66 13s. 4d. This money went to the Lord's successor and in mediæval times it would have been no light sum. It had to be paid within five years and in return the tenants were granted full rights of Common in the Manorial waste.

Having dealt with the feudal payments the Jury set out the customary arrangements for holding the manorial courts of Wentllwg, the procedure for issuing writs in them and the legal fees due to the attorneys, the Stewards, the Recorders and the Bailiffs. The Juries impanelled at the manorial courts received one shilling if they merely had to attend court and decide a suit between two parties : if on the other hand their duty for the day was to " view watercourses, find rights of way, and part hedges," in other words to decide a disputed boundary, they received two shillings. The duty of deciding boundaries is a clear survival of the original function of English Juries, a function coming down to us from the courts of the Anglo-Saxons and perhaps even earlier than that. The English jury of the last few centuries has been called to the courts to decide, as a body of fair and honest men, upon a case that is put before them and of which they have no previous knowledge. The function of the primitive jury was to act as a body of neighbour-witnesses, to testify to a fact which they as the local inhabitants might be supposed to know better than anyone else.

A list was then appended of the feudal rents paid by the free tenants. The largest of these was £1 14s. 8d., paid by Sir Thomas Kemeys for the " demesne of Vaindre in the possession of Thomas Watkins, gent." ; the next was a payment of 14s. 4d. made by Thomas Morgan for the holding of Tredegar.

Lastly the jury made an effort at setting out the list of cottages. There were not very many in 1700—only 14 were listed and the rents of these could not be had except by reference to the Lord's books to see what was usually paid. At the end of the Survey were placed the signatures of those members of the panel who could write and the curious marks and splodges of those who could not.

This, in its last stages with its feudal rents and payments shrunk almost to nothing, was the mediaeval organization of the lordship of Wentllwg. It held good in all the manors save the five mentioned above, of which the most important was Bassaleg.

Here then is the custom of the Manor of Bassaleg as set out in its own Court of Survey, held at the house of Anne Watkins in Bassaleg on October 10th, 1720.

THE MANOR OF BASSALEG.
PRESENTMENT OF JURY OF SURVEY AT COURT BARON AND COURT OF SURVEY, 1720.

" To the First Article we present that the Manor or Lordship of Bassaleg in the County of Monmouth aforesaid hath for its means and bounds the Lordship of Wentlooge and the Manors of Abercarne, Rogerstone and Dufferin, and lyeth in the several Parishes of St. Woolos, Risca, St. Brides, Peterstone and Bassaleg, in the County aforesaid and that the Bishop of Llandaff is for the time being the true and undoubted Lord of the said Manor, and the same is now held in lease by the Honourable James Bertie, Esq., and the Honourable Dodington Grenville as trustees of the most noble Henry Duke of Beaufort granted for them by the Rt. Rev. Father in God, John, now Lord Bishop of Llandaff aforesaid."*

" We present to the Second Article that there are two sorts of tenure of land within the Lordship of Bassaleg and both customary and held by the Virge and that

---

* The Bishop was John Tyler, Dean of Hereford, Bishop of Llandaff, 1706-1724.

all the lands lying within the said Lordship within the several parishes of St. Woolos, St. Brides, Peterston and the lower part of Bassaleg are Borough English tenure and do hereditarily descend to the youngest son and for want of a son the youngest daughter and for want of a daughter the youngest next of kin ; and that all the lands within the said Lordship that lie within the said Parish of Risca and the upper part of the Parish of Bassaleg are of Gavelkind tenure and descend between all sons and for want of sons all the daughters and for want of them all the next of kin in like manner ; and none of the tenants of the said Manor forfeit their land to the Lord thereof for any manner of fact whatsoever. Only we find that Rowland Rees held three acres of land at St. Brides, late the land of Sir Anthony Morgan, by Common Law Conveyance and has been so transferred time out of mind."

Since the 12th Century the usual mode of descent of land in England has been that of Primogeniture-descent to the eldest son. Gavelkind, descent to all sons equally, was a rarity in England but was the normal mode in Wales until Henry VIII's Act of Union. Borough English was another variation legalized by ancient usage in which descent was to the youngest son and, with Gavelkind, it was abolished in 1925.

The Third Article of Presentment declared that tenants owed suit and service at Courts Baron, Courts Leet and Hallmoot provided that the Lord held Courts Leet in May and Michaelmas and Courts Baron not more than once in three weeks. Hallmoot for surrender of land could be held as often as need required. For absence from Hallmoot and Court Baron the tenant incurred a Fine of 39s. 11d. which the Steward might lower to not less than 6s. 8d. Absence from Court Leet is " in the brest of the Assessory and the fine of every Resciant their default of Appearance shall be 4d. no more or less."

To the Fourth Article they presented that Fines
Heriots, Reliefs, and Alieniations were, (1) for tenants
holding the land in Gavelkind tenure, a Heriot of the
best beast at the death of the tenant or if he had no
cattle depasturing then 5s. in lieu thereof.   If a Gavelkind
tenant alienated all his estate an Alienation of 5s. had to
be paid but if he sold part and kept part there was no
payment.   (2) Tenants in Borough English had to pay
an Alienation or Descent payment rated at 6s. 7d. per Acre
and a Heriot as in Gavelkind.

In the Fifth Article they presented that a widow in
the Manor of Bassaleg held during her widowhood and
continued all that estate of which her husband had been
seized in Borough English tenure and one third of that
which he had held in Gavelkind.   The husband of an
heiress in Gavelkind held one third for his life if she
died without issue by him, but if she left issue, dead
or alive, he held all.

The Sixth Article pointed out that tenants owed no
suit to other Courts, and that the Lord had a right of
hawking, hunting and fowling.   The Lord also owned
absolutely the goods of all Felons, Wayfes, Estrayes,
Deodands, Forfeitures of Goods and Treasure Trove,
also Escheats of all lands and tenements of which a
tenant died seized without heirs special or general, of
Bastards dying without issue.   If any tenant of this
Manor Alieneth his land by Common Law Conveyance
out of the Court of this Manor he shall forfeit the same
to the Lord."

In the Seventh Article they presented that the Lord
had two Commons ; the one called The Garth, the other
called The Little Common.   Tenants had freedom
there with all their commonable cattle ; the Lord had
his rights there and anyone but tenants and resciants
who pastured there was liable to a fine.

" To the Eighth Article we present that there is a

Pound in the Village of Bassaleg and the profit therefrom is to the Lord let out at 6s. 8d. per annum. The Fee for each impounding is 1d. for every tenant and 4d. for every foreigner."

This Fee was paid for the release of the animal which had strayed and been impounded. The idea of a " foreigner " from, say, Machen, or St. Brides, is delightful.

The Ninth Article presented a list of the lands and their chief rents. Most of the names are now unrecognisable, except for " Kae Cross Inin," (Croes Carn Einion) and " Ruer Derin " (Rhiwderin). Kae Cross Inin was in the possession of William Edward Rees at 5d. Harry Meyrick held Ruer Derin at 1s. 0d., while the Vicarage rented at 5d. These were of course not the real rents but only the manorial chief rents.

The Tenth Article presented " Encroachments of land " on the Garth and the lands waste by the Churchyard. " That Anne Watkins has encroached a house, garden and outhouse on Garth Common."

To the Eleventh Article they stated that nobody was to be Reeve or Deputy unless he had land to the value of the chief rent. The Reeve and Deputy were to be chosen by the Michaelmas Leet Jury ; Borough English Tenants were not to hold office more than once in three years ; Gavelkind tenants not more than two yeers out of three. The Lords Chief Rent was £6 13s. 4d. The Steward's fee was to be £1 0s. 0d. for every Surrender of Land. The tenants were to get £1 0s. 0d. or their dinner for attending every Hallmoot Court. For swearing each tenant, the Steward and Bailiff got 6d. apiece, for summoning each Juryman the Bailiff got 4d., and for every warrant and likewise for the copy of every surrender the Steward got 7s. 6d., besides parchment and stamps.

The survey was signed by

Marmaduke Griffith (Steward)
Wm. Morgan of Malpas
Trevor Harry
Wm. Morgan of Bassaleg
John Isaac
Wm. Evans
Ed. Lewis
Ed. Llewellin
Wm. Thomas
Lewis Harry

The Beauforts did not hold the manor for long because on May 2nd, 1736, " Thomas Morgan of Rhiwperra, Lord of the Manor of Bassaleg, grants at his pleasure the rights to hold his courts, to hold office as Steward and to take profits therefrom to Charles Phillips of Gellibear in Monmouthshire." On the 6th June, 1736, Court Baron was " holden at the house of Richard Ellis the freeholder at Nine of the clock " and Charles Phillips made Thomas Bryan his Deputy.

Other Stewards in the century were :—

1749   Thomas Bryan, William Thomas
1773   Hugh Evans
1777   Evan Phillips

Thomas Morgan was succeeded by his son John, on whose death in 1792 the familiar name of Sir Charles Morgan, Baronet, of Tredegar appears at the foot of the rolls of Admittances and Surrenders of land. This gentleman was Sir Charles Gould of Little Ealing Middlesex, Knight, Judge Advocate General of H.M. Forces. He had married Jane (died 1797) eldest sister of John Morgan and when she succeeded to the Estates of her brother in 1792 he took her name. Sir Charles' son became the better known Sir Charles Morgan of the nineteenth century and it was his son, the third Sir Charles, who became the first Baron Tredegar.

In 1800 Thomas Rosser became Steward and before long the Admittance to land held in Copyhold became entirely a legal form and it seems that the solicitor acted as Steward.

MAESGLAS

While dealing with the Tredegar manors it would be as well to preserve on record the custom of another one—that called " Greenfield " in the Wentllwg survey of 1700.   The manor of Greenfield, to-day known by its Welsh equivalent " Maesglas," was the mediaeval Ebboth and was from very early times a part of the Duchy of Lancaster.   The diary of Richard Symonds, who accompanied Charles I, recorded in 1645 that of castles in Monmouthshire some were habitable, others were ruined but that Tregwillim and Greenfield had disappeared.   There was indeed a small castle in this place but it had not entirely vanished since Coxe noticed one tower being used as a stable in the buildings of old Maesglas farm.   The farm now stands in the grounds of Maesglas school but of the castle not a trace remains. As with Gwern y Cleppa, Greenfield was marked as a village on Saxton's map of 1570, with the result that as far as the London mapmakers were concerned it remained a village until well into the eighteenth century.

In the late fifteenth century this manor was occupied by Henry Kemeys, coroner of Wentllwg, who was dead by 1533.

In the manor of Greenfield, which lay in the parishes of St. Woolos, St. Brides and Peterstone, lands descended to the youngest son of the first wife and the heirs of his body and in default then to the second son.   In default of sons by the first wife the daughters took like brothers in degree of age.   If there were no daughters then the land was taken by the youngest son of the second wife.

When a freehold tenant died a heriot of 5s. had to be

paid and there was in this manor a Relief to be paid consisting of one year's rent. If a customary tenant alienated part of his land he had to make a payment rated at 2s. an acre and if he sold the whole he also had to pay a heriot of 5s. ; if he died similar payments had to be made out of his estate. If a man married an heiress of land and she died, a heriot of 5s. had to be paid and the man then held all the land during his life. Widows and widowers were liable to forfeit their land if they committed wilful waste of its substance. Customary fineable land was rented at 4½d. an acre.

While these records are of most interest to those historically interested in manorial affairs, they afford a glimpse of an earlier agricultural society and of a different Wentllwg which should not, I feel, be allowed to sink into unrecorded oblivion.

CHAPTER IX.

MODERN BASSALEG.

WE have been with Wentllwg throughout its ages and now we are on the threshold of the industrial revolution and the modern world. For this area, as for so much of the country, this meant a fourfold increase in population with the arrival of scientific development of industry and vastly improved methods of transport and communication.

GROWTH OF POPULATION.

The latter half of the eighteenth and the beginning of the nineteenth centuries brought many buildings that we know to-day, although the exact dates of most of them are impossible to ascertain. Old Bassaleg House and Fairoak are certainly of the eighteenth century, as are one house in Pen y Lan, the old police station, and the Tredegar Arms. In the later part of the period appeared places such as Ffos y Fran, Croes Carn Einion, Rogerstone Castle House and the turnpike house on the corner of Forge Lane that survived till the lane gave place to an eighty foot carriageway. Various thatched cottages by the Church Hall, in Pentrepoeth and elsewhere were built at this time and so were many others which have already disappeared such as those in Pool Sands, in Fairoak Wall, by Ffynnon Oer barn and opposite the Elementary School. The Baptist Chapel was built in 1832.

Various houses of the agricultural type were constructed in Pen y Lan, the Griffin, and Pentrepoeth during the middle of the century and, not long after, industrial

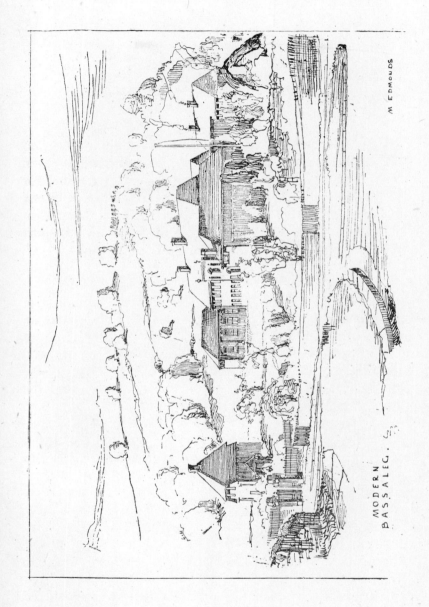

MODERN
BASSALEG.

M EDMONDS

workers dwellings were built up Garth Hill and the lower end of Pentrepoeth. The coach houses were built in 1843, the Wesleyan Chapel in 1873, and there was a Congregational Chapel on the site of the present wheelwright's shop that was still a place of worship as late as 1884. In the last years of the century came houses between the bridge and Pye Corner, Brynhedydd, Ysgubor Goch and of course the unpleasant Victorian architecture of the unsightly Highfield Villas. The later spread of the village is all too obvious to require mention in this book.

INDUSTRY.

Industry came many years before modern transport. The railway did not come up from Newport till the middle of the century, but when Coxe walked the county there was already a charcoal forge in Tredegar Park and another at Machen both belonging to Harford, Partridge and Co. The Forge in Bassaleg gave its name to Forge Lane and got its sand from the pits at Pool Sands. Rogerstone Castle at this time housed a tin plate works. The canal was constructed above the Cefn quite early in the century and a rail road for horse-drawn trucks ran down from the valleys to Newport carrying the coal from the mines which were then being opened in great numbers. In the midst of a cold, grey, early morning of November, 1839, the Chartist host must have passed through Rogerstone and Bassaleg on the way to the disastrous attempt to capture Newport. It was not in that fashion nor, alas, so soon that decent conditions and elementary justice were to be secured for working people in South Wales.

ROGERSTONE CASTLE.

When Coxe in 1800 came to speak of Rogerstone Castle he described it much as it is to-day. " The only remains

of the ancient structure are visible in the walls and
outhouses of the present mansion which is a modern
edifice built on old foundations.   These fragments are
very massive and measure without their facings near
seven feet in thickness, they occupy a Mount which was
the site of the ancient citidal.   The field adjoining the
garden is still called Castle Close.   The premises as
well as some adjoining works on the bank of the Ebbw
belong to the Royal Mine Company and are tenanted
by Mr. Butler of Caerleon.   They were erected in 1772
for Copper Works but are now used for the manufacture
of iron rods, bars, bolts for shipping, and tin plates."
   What more is there to add ?   From 1772 onwards
factory followed factory till in this last decade we have
seen the Castle Steel Works give way to a newer industry
still.   The Mound is there, the whitewashed Castle
house is there, the massive fragments can still be seen
in the stable wall by anyone standing on the road.
   There is one tale in the village concerning Rogerstone
Castle.   Many years ago a man called Leafroy—there
are several people who remember him—had the use of
the stable.   Finding that the drainage disappeared with
unusual speed he traced it to the edge of an old stone.
After bending several bars, he and a friend raised the
slab and there before them lay the traditional steps and
secret tunnel.   They went along it for several hundred
yards but the atmosphere became too foul to continue.
The stableyard is now tiled and I was told that the drain
there " carries the water to an old Sump ". . . . . We
must leave it without comment as a splendid possibility
and there too we must leave the ancient Castle of Rogerstone or Tre Gwilym.

BASSALEG CHURCH.

We find an apt description of the modern Church in
the indefatigable Coxe.   If the worthy Archdeacon had

but lived in an age when Archæology had become a science, instead of being a jungle of absurd legend, there would have been little to add to his history to-day. It is the starting point of any investigation into any part of the County, a veritable Gwentian Encyclopædia.

" The present Church " he says " is a neat Gothic edifice . . . . A few years ago it was repaired and so much altered that it bears few traces of its original style.   It appears from the sepulchral inscriptions that the collateral branches of the Morgan family seated at Gwern y Cleppa and Rogerstone were buried in the church.   Jane, eldest sister of the late John Morgan, Esq., of Tredegar, the wife of Sir Charles Gould Morgan is interred in a cemetery lately erected by her husband who transferred the burial place of the Tredegar family from Machen to this church.   A small Gothic edifice now a Schoolroom stands a few paces from the South side of the Church and was probably an ancient chapel."

The picture in Coxe shows the church much as we see it to-day, and quite " neat " it still is despite the somewhat lopsided appearance presented by those Decorated churches which have a single aisle on the south side.   But alas, Coxe's opening words are only too true. The Church has been restored out of all recognition. Succeeding generations of benefactors have repaired the church in contemporary taste so that nothing but its external fabric is of the least architectural or historical interest.   It was in that state in 1800 and there have been several major reconstructions since !

Externally the walls and windows are of the Decorated period of church architecture, with the exception of the East window and Chancel which are Perpendicular.   We cannot safely date any of it before 1250 and some perhaps as late as 1400, but supposing most of the fabric to have been built at one time then the late Decorated Bar Tracery of the Nave, together with the later East and

Tower windows would lead us to suppose that the church was built in the transitional Decorated-Perpendicular period of English Gothic architecture, about the middle of the 14th century. The Porch seems to be modern, or entirely reconstructed and the number of ornaments appearing in it, heads and suchlike, have clearly come off the old structure. The Arch is of the Decorated period and may have been moved from the original doorway and reconstructed. The springers of the original Main door-arch show clearly beside the present somewhat severe—not to say ugly entrance.

The fine Lych gate at the entrance to the Churchyard is modern being the War Memorial of the Civic Parish of Graig.

The interior is of even less interest than the exterior with stone refaced, walls cream plastered, window ledges chiselled, arches reconstructed, pillars reshaped, side chapel renewed, and piscina remoulded. A church of fine proportions and neat appearance but of negative architectural value.

The stained glass of the East Window is of the most vulgar period of 19th Century glass work, indeed, the glass of the whole church is redeemed solely by the soft colouring of the very fine window opposite the Main door to the memory of Lieutenant-Colonel Joseph Wilkie and the Officers and men of the 17th Battn., the Welch Regiment, who fell in the First Great War. In the Nave there is a splendid pair of brass candelabra of date 1822 bearing the inscription "A gift of the Rev. Arthur Allett Isaacson, Vicar of this Parish Church of Newport alias St. Woolos." It is not clear at what date or why St. Woolos bestowed them on Bassaleg.

A Cross from the grave of some Unknown soldier who died in France, presented to Bassaleg by the War Graves Commission in March 1930 is also of interest. There is a fine modern Reredos donated by Miss Hanmer of Rogerstone and the Lectern was given by Edmund Watts in 1890.*

It was a failing of Victorian restorers to smother their churches with inartistic pitch-pine pews, ill carved pulpits, or elaborate brass lecterns and with this furniture they filled up their Naves. The Nave of the average parish church was floored with the gravestones of the 16th, 17th and early 18th centuries and in some cases these were removed and erected elsewhere. This was not done in Bassaleg and we are confronted in the Nave and Chancel with tantalizing portions of the tombstones of former generations of Bassaleg people that we cannot read. Who knows what interesting or attractive stones, what coats of arms or Epitaphs do not lie under these pews ; pews without which we should realize the spaciousness and proportion of Bassaleg— indeed of every other church—so much better ; pews which in this case are covered with a disfiguring light stain and varnish.

With the exception of Roger Morgan who died in July, 1633, and lies with his wife on the South side of the Altar we have no tombs of the branch from Gwern y Cleppa which Coxe mentioned as being buried at Bassaleg. As regards Rogerstone Castle there is no sign of Morgan of Rogerstone to be found anywhere with with the exception of " John Morgan of Rogerstone in the parish of Bassalegg in ye county of Monmouth, yeoman," who died in 1677. As we have seen Rogerstone was held in 1700 by Edmund Morgan of Penllwyn Sarph and he may have succeeded his relative, John.

There is also a tomb of a Family called Halliday, who were occupying Rogerstone Castle House towards the end of the 18th century, probably before Mr.

---

* The excellent pulpit was presented by Mr. and Mrs. A. R. Jones of Sunnybank, Rhiwderin, in memory of their son, Basil Rees Jones who died in 1935.

Butler and the Tin Works mentioned by Coxe.

The burial ground of the senior branch of the Morgans was transferred from Machen by Sir Charles Gould Morgan and in this century the side chapel was erected to house the modern tombstones, the older ones being left at Lower Machen.

The lesser branches of the Family had, however, always been buried at Bassaleg. For instance Margaret wife of John Morgan of Gelynos Fawr who died on January 5th, 1797, at the age of 89. On the same stone but attaching to some earlier Morgan whose name is hidden by a piece of furniture, is the following epitaph :

" The stroke of death did end my time
And cut me off just in my prime
Short was my life
Great was my pain
Great was your loss
Great was my gain."

The old Morgan tombs around the Chancel and Sanctuary of Bassaleg church, untrodden by the congregation, unspoilt by furniture—merely carpeted—are in an excellent state of preservation.

The hatchments over the arches of the Nave pillars, although bearing fine Coats of Arms, have unfortunately not the inscriptions which are on the similar Morgan hatchments at Lower Machen Church.

Since the mid-18th century with the exception of the Tredegar wall tablets and those of the Homfray Family (who also have the fine solid square tomb, in the classical style, near the church door) few sepulchral monuments have gone inside the church.

Lastly Coxe mentions the small Gothic building in what is now the middle of the churchyard. This is clearly shown in his picture and its disappearance is recorded in the Archæologia Cambrensis (January, 1859). " We have been informed that a small isolated

Perpendicular building, a Chapel in Bassaleg Church-yard, detached from the Church, has lately been destroyed by action of the incumbent and owner of the Rectorial tithes. We regret this, for although it has been used as a Schoolroom for some time past, detached chapels are by no means common and this one might have been preserved." It was clearly the original Church School, for whose Schoolmaster Rowland Morgan gave £20 in 1675.

This seems an apt place to set out in full the list of Incumbents of St. Basil's, as given in the church, and presumably taken from records at Llandaff.

1069   Benedictus.

1140   Helias.

1397   Dafydd ap Hywel May 1397 (Canon of Llandaff April 1398).

1535   Sir Roger Griffith.

1542   Henry Morgan.

1556   Lewis Rees (Instituted by the Archbishop).

1578 June 18   William Blethin, LL.B., BCL. Canon of Llandaff 1553. Archdeacon of Brecon 1567. Bishop of Llandaff 1585.

1591 May 27   Morgan Blethin. Appointed by Queen Elizabeth, Canon of Llandaff 1603.

1623 May 28   Theophilus Field. Bishop of Llandaff 1623. Bishop of St. Davids 1627. Bishop of Hereford 1635.

1624 May 31   George Watkins, B.A.

1663 Feb. 28   John Jones.

1673 Aug. 26   John Watkins—Canon of Llandaff 1672

1690 Oct. 6   Richard Yorath, M.A.

1699 Feb. 18   George Williams, B.A.

1729 Nov.   John Robotham, B.A. (Appointed by the King).

1763 July 5   Wyndham Lewis, M.A.

1782 Feb. 2   Thomas Leyshon, M.A.   Canon of
                Llandaff 1812.
1823 March 3   Hugh Williams, Canon of Llandaff 1837
1877   William Watkins.
1878 Feb. 5   John Jones, B.A., died December 25th,
                1897.
1898 April 26 David Bowen, B.A.
1925 Sept. 19 John Griffith Matthias, B.A., Rural
                Dean of Bassaleg September 3rd,
                1927, Canon of Monmouth October
                3rd 1930.
1931 March 5   George Morgannwg William Thomas
                Jenkins.
1934 March 13 Alfred Gwilym Arthur Picton, B.A.,
                M.C., Rural Dean of Bassaleg 1943.

To this list we must add Roger de Novo Burgo
who, as we saw in chapter 5, was appointed in 1190-91.

Now the most interesting of these our Vicars was
undoubtedly Theophilus Field (1623-24).*   He was
chaplain to Sir Francis Bacon, and later to the King's
favourite, the Duke of Buckingham, who in 1619 secured
for him the Bishopric of Llandaff.   He had, however,
assisted Bacon in corrupt practices and in 1621 was
impeached before Parliament for bribery and brocage
and censured by Archbishop Abbot in Convocation.
Nothing but a wealthier see than Llandaff could heal
this blow to his pride and for several years he addressed
begging letters to Buckingham pleading with fawning
sycophancy to be translated to Hereford. " My Lord,
I am grown an old man and am like old household-stuff
—apt to be broke on often removing. I desire it therefore but once for all, be it Ely or Bath and Wells and
I will spend the remainder of my days writing an history
of your good deeds to me and others . . . "

---

* A full account of Theophilus Field is given in " Archbishop Laud " by
H. R. Trevor Roper. Macmillan, 1940.

DUFFRYN EBBW.

H. EDMONDS.

Poor Theophilus ! He was given not the splendid Hereford but the far-distant, windswept St. Davids. Pleading ill health he continued to hang around Westminster, only visiting his new diocese once when his sole pastoral achievement was to get the cathedral whitewashed. At last in 1635, six years after Buckingham had been assassinated, authority smiled on Field and he was sent to die in Hereford. He must have taken Bassaleg during his disgrace, solely to draw its revenues.

The Parish almshouse was Bay-Tree Cottage on the left of the road between Bassaleg and Garth. This house bears on its outer wall an inscribed stone which reads " Houses erected by the inhabitants of the parish of Duffrin for their poor in the year 1816." At some time the house ceased to fulfil its original function and came into Tredegar hands.

In 1859, John Seys and David Davies, churchwardens, signed the notice of benefactions that now hangs inside the church, above the door. Seys, derived from Saes, meaning a Saxon or Englishman is a common name in South Wales and still survives in Bassaleg.

Such is the place of worship of the Parish of Bassaleg, a worthy place that is still, as it has been for 1500 years, the Mother Church of the Cantref of Wentllwg.

BASSALEG'S RIVER.

The name of the river on which the Parish is situated is spelt Ebbw at the present day, although it could be spelt Ebwy until quite recent years. So late a work as the " Times Atlas " of 1922 has the word Ebwy ; although Ebbw Vale is the spelling it gives to the town at the head of the valley. The De Clare surveys of 1295 and 1314. have it Ebboth, Leland has it Ebowith, Speed, gives Ebwith. Clearly the Welsh original termination was—wydd which the English tried originally to spell Woth and With—inaccurately as usual. It is not unknown in Welsh for a final dd to be dropped and a century ago it was colloquially pronounced Ebbw, an obvious spoken variation of the written Ebwy—itself a contraction of Ebwydd.

Alas for Bassaleg ! It is nearly a century and a half since the clear torrent sparkling between the red rocky banks, delighted the early nineteenth century travellers. It is over a hundred years since last it threw its clear mountain water under the old pack-horse bridge, reflecting the church tufted in the trees that so enchanted Coxe and Donovan. We who live in the Vale have to suffer for what man has permitted industrial enterprise to do in the high mountains. The rivers should be for the people's use, they should be clear as God's rain that falls on the mountains that feed them. Afon Llwyd, Ebbw, Sirhowy, Rhymni, Taf, what have they done to you ? They have killed you and everything in you, Whatever benefit someone has derived from this desolation was bought at a terrible price and it is we who live on your banks must pay it.

TRAVELLERS.

Donovan, Coxe, Barber and Pennant, travellers, all came to Wales when the French Wars prevented the Grand Tour of Europe. Coxe we have mentioned on many occasions, while Barber seems to have such an an inordinately long section on Monmouthshire for a book of no great size, covering all South Wales, that I suspect him of taking much of it word for word from Coxe.

Donovan passed us by on Cardiff Road saying " There is a view of singular beauty deserving mention in which a little extent of Country is seen smiling in all the pride of rural neatness. The distance is closed by an appropriate boundary of hills, the church of Basileg rearing its aged Front in one point of the view among trees, a few whitened cottages are also visible and the whole produce an effect of mild, simple and unaffected beauty." One has only to stand in part of Tredegar Park to realise that Donovan was, if anything, understating the extraordinary beauty of the lower Ebbw Valley looking towards the splendid escarpment of Mynydd Henllys, and Mynydd Maen. Lower Wentllwg is full of splendid views of hill and valley—for those prepared to do some walking.

In the Autumn of 1854 a more famous figure came down the Caerphilly Road. He wore a dog collar and carried a haversack; he had come out of Wales and was nearing the end of a long journey, very weary. George Borrow, for it was none other, found Bassaleg a pleasant village standing in a valley, nearly surrounded by the groves of Sir Charles Morgan. Seeing a decent public house " I think, I shall have my ale here and not go running after Sir Charles who perhaps after all I shouldn't find at home. Over my ale I trifled for about half an hour then paying my groat I got up and set off for Newport in the midst of a thick mist which had suddenly come on and speedily wetted me to the skin."

Where was the respectable public house ? The Ruperra Arms was probably not built and even if it was it had no license even as late as 1884. There must at one time have been an inn by the cluster of houses below Fairoak—else it is difficult to see why they are called " The Griffiin "—but it would have been off Borrow's road. The Tredegar Arms seems to be the most natural place for the thirsty traveller to have gone to get his ale. It is often said, however, that the old police station opposite Bassaleg House was once an inn and if that is so then it, too, may have some claim to have been the alehouse that took Borrow's groat.

Licensed houses are transitory things. There was one

in 1884 called the " Three Horseshoes " not far from the present " Three Salmons " and " Bush " but in those days, before the advent of the " tied " house or the large brewery combines, an alehouse was often nothing more than a cottage with a license to brew and sell. As such, when it gave up its license, it might speedily be forgotten.

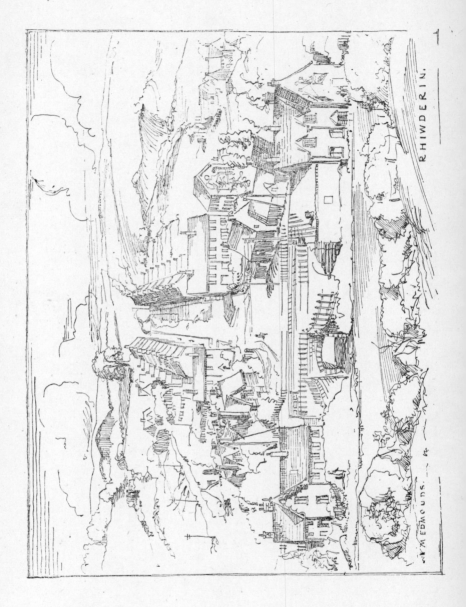

RHIWDERIN.

W. MEDWOUDS.

CHAPTER X.

" RHIWDERIN AND TYDU."

RHIWDERIN.

A T first sight " Rhiwderin " appears to be a perfectly
simple name. Unfortunately there are two possible
derivations and it is impossible and perhaps unnecessary
to decide between them. The name is nowadays spelt
Rhiwderin or Rhiwderyn, and Rhiw we know means the
slope of a hill. Derwen is an Oak Tree ; aderyn is a
Bird but its plural is adar. I would say that the first
alternative provides the most probable origin. One oak
is more likely on the slope of a hill than one bird !

Rhiwderin Iron Age Fort has already been mentioned
in Chapter II and lands held in Ruer Derin in Chapter
VII. There is only one other reference to the place in
old records. The third son of Rowland Morgan of
Gwern y Cleppa living in 1604-1628, was called Edward.
Edward's daughter was Barbara Morgan, and she married
Matthew Morgan of " Rhywderin." Rhiwderin has no
noticeably ancient buildings and I suggest that Matthew
lived in Glochwen Farm. The west side is comparatively
modern, but the back might possibly be as old as
the mid-17th Century. Some building may have stood
there even if the present structure is only of the
18th Century.

Rhiwderin then has very little ancient history ; it is
called a mere hamlet of Bassaleg. Anyone knowing
Rhiwderin, however, can testify that that uninhabited
stretch of road under Garth Wood makes all the difference

as between two villages.   Turn Garth Corner and there
is Garth House whose front part was still a farm about
1880.   Much reconstructed, it is of some but very
uncertain age, probably not above one hundred and
twenty years.   There ahead is Rhiwderin, a comparatively
modern place.   Houses, school, chapel, station are all of
much the same age.   The Inn is probably of earlier
construction, but again its age is doubtful.   It is now
the sole licensed house, the old Maypole, Carpenters
Arms, and Vulcan having, like the Inn at Lower Machen
and the Hollybush at Draethen, become mere dwelling
houses.   For a small population such as Rhiwderin had
before the Street was built there must have been plenty
of beer !

There were old cottages in various places, such as
those below Foxwood, on the side of the lane between
Rhiwderin and Pump Heol and between the crest of
Coed Mawr and Llandanglws.   In addition there is talk
of a row of Nailmakers cottages, which are supposed to
have led up the hill from Pentre Tai Farm ; Pentre
Tai means " The Village of Houses," so the story is
quite probable.

In the middle of the Nineteenth Century arrived the
Rhiwderin Tin Plate Company.   Mr. Robert Nourse
its Manager, regrettably enough, saw fit to deface the
top of the old Garth Common, now cultivated, as Highfield Hill, with his two yellow brick mansions.   The cost
was as fantastic as their appearance and possibly this
contributed to the fairly rapid end of the Tin Works
which, by 1895 or before, had become the Tredegar
Yard.   The Tin Works still remain in the building
housing Periam's Brush Factory, in pits in the earth
and grass covered slag.   The old office stands on the
roadside by the tunnel under the railway.

The bricks for the street came from pits dug beyond
the Village beside the Iron Age Fort Hill.

There are two lanes from Rhiwderin to the Michaelstone Road. One goes past Brynhedydd and is now
called Coc y North. It is named after a farm called Coc
y North which lay by the lane opposite the barn and
bungalow now standing on the left. Scarcely one stone
of the farm remains. The other lane is called Cwm
Cwdy or possibly Cwm Cwty. This is a doubtful name.
Cwta means short or possibly " a short cut." The
Six-Inch Map refers to it as Cwm Dylluan—the valley
of the Owl—and I would dismiss this as mere Ordnance
moonshine were it not that an old Manorial admittance
refers to a lane called " Cwm Drellian "—a Lane " running between Rhiwderin and Croescarneinion." Now
it is obvious that the direct lane between Rhiwderin
and Croescarneinion is not Cwm Cwdy but Coc y
North, and it is impossible to suppose that Coc y North
is a modern lane because although Ysgubor Wen and
Brynhedydd are modern houses, Coc y North Farm and
Pen y Groes Cottage are very old. It is clearly the
document which is at fault, since Cwm Cwdy lies in its
own little " Cwm." Not for many years has the " Short
Valley " been known as the haunt of the bird of night.

Just by Rhiwderin station in the road side is a fine
block of stone and whichever side a writer takes on the
subject of this and other stones in the area, he is sure
to bring down heaped coals of fire on his luckless head.
There is a deep rooted local tradition of Boundary
Stones and Markers ; a local belief that these stones
point somewhere or mean something. In any convser-
sation on this subject somebody will mention either a
new stone or a new theory about them. They are all
cut on the same side, one man will say ; another assures
us that they are part of a vast system of prehistoric
boundaries or that they mark an old road ; yet another
declares that this Rhiwderin Stone points to the Iron
Age Fort. There is a big stone below Bryn Rhos in

the brook side ; there is one nearly opposite Brynhedydd gate in the road bank—one can hear of a score more around the district. It so happens that we are here on the sandstone, but two miles West and North West runs the belt of lime-stone, barely half a mile wide, which is the rim of the great saucer of lime-stone running under the South Wales coal measures. It is marked in a thin blue line on the geological maps and goes right around the coal area. It passes near Lower Machen and Pont y Mister, going over the shoulder of Mynydd Machen above Llandanglws in a welter of tumbled, white-speckled, millstone grit, known as The Devils Apron Strings. For look you now as the Devil was carrying material to help build Monmouth Bridge he tripped, and, breaking his apron string, spilt the stone !

The Millstone grit was, to a certain extent, carried down to the sandstone measures in the later Ice Age by glacial drift, leaving deposit which in later ages was worn into manageable boulders. Farmers are always ploughing these up and the copse containing the rise of Bassaleg Brook above Croesheolydd is full of them. Some of these stones are more studded with white pebbles than others. Rhiwderin stone is not studded at all.

I refuse to support the idea that these stones mean anything as a whole, though, in the solitary case, Rhiwderin Stone might have been cut to its extraordinary shape for some purpose, e.g. a mile stone. A hole has definitely been tooled in it at some period. The others are all blocks of Millstone Grit which have been ploughed up after the soil has worn down to them and then cast into the hedge by some irate farmer or else they are still lying where the glaciers left them. If there are any serious supporters of the " mystery meaning " or " Marker " theory then I ask them, what did they mark ? What people in what age put them there ?

There is a far more fascinating idea on which to dwell, in another part of Rhiwderin. When the Reverend John Griffiths, of Nantymoel, wrote his book " Edward II. in Glamorgan" he had a chapter on " The Little People of Glamorgan." " The Little People " are none other than the Tylwyth Teg, the Fair Folk ; in English they are called the Lordly Ones of The Hollow Hills, the Fairies who dwell in the depths of the Mountains. John Griffiths' delightful chapter recalls some possible place names coupled with the Old Ones. He finds them in most of South Wales, but here a sudden outcrop occurs on the mountain edge between Pontypool and Cardiff. There are many Ty Pwca's, the Houses of Puck, the Abodes of the Master Goblin himself ; one is beyond Henllys and Castell y Bwch, one is in Cwm Bran, one in Pont y Mister, one on the mountain top above Machen Upper. There is Llwyn y Bwbach between the Sirhowy and Cefn Bedwellty—the Goblin's Bush. There is a whole string of names connected with a race of Dwarf's and little people :—Coed y Gorres at Llanedyrn means the She-Dwarf's wood, Ty Grwca the Humpback's House and Gwern y Eiddil the Weakling's Meadow, are near Coed y Corres. Nant y Cor, the Dwarf's Brook runs into the Rhymni, from Rhiwperra Castle. The writer then recalls a small cottage in Aberdare called Castell y Corryn, the Dwarf's Castle, a name which he says is proverbial there for a minute house. " There are small dwellings everywhere and one wonders if the same is to be found in other parishes." Alas for John Griffiths ! He went to Llangwm from Nantymoel ; he never came to Rhiwderin or we could have shown him. Above Pentre Tai and its now vanished row of Nailmaker's dwellings by the hedgerow below Fox Wood are the remains of a small cottage. This place is called Castell y Corryn. Crops grow taller over old foundations and higher wheat is the only evidence of buildings lower down but this has clearly been a house. The ruins are still there.

One may not believe in the Beautiful Ones very strongly, some do, some don't, but it is poor imagination that can walk in a wood at night when the owl cries and the dark pool is still or can look up on to the vast bare shoulder of the mountain, cold and silver in the moonlight, or black and tossed in a rising wind and not wonder if the mountain and the trees are perhaps, after all, not quite alone ; if there is not more in the night than mortal eye may see. Maybe we with our noise have driven the little people out of Wentllwg, where surely they belong, but the recesses of Mynydd Maen are still quiet enough even for them.

TYDU.

Tydu and Tre Gwillim are the two parts of Rogerstone, above the Railway which are all modern. Of Tre Gwillim, by the Castle, we have spoken. The various factories at the Castle brought a number of houses there from about 1790 onwards and linked it up with Tydu both along the main road and under the the bank where the footpath leads over the river to Rhiwderin. Tydu House is a large structure of the late 18th or early 19th century used as a Recreation Building. There are also a number of old cottages and there was, until a few years ago, an old Nail Works by the Rhiwderin Path. Ugly it may have been, but it was a beauty spot compared to its successor !

Along the level water meadows is Pont Newydd Fawr farm—not to be confused with Pont Newydd Fach, a smaller, more recent, building on the Rhiwderin side of the river. Pont Newydd Fawr is very fine ; one side is in the style of Croesheolydd but the front of the house has something more of the William and Mary or Anne period about it. Whether this is added or the house is a late example of one and an early example of the other it is imposssble to say without a detailed examination of the interior which has not been undertaken. It is a very attractive, well proportioned building.

Finally, there is the local Bard. There was an old man in the later nineteenth century who lived at Tydu. He wrote Verse—to call it Poetry would be to dignify it to excess, but it rhymed and it often scanned and it provides a mine of apparently unconscious humour to those lucky enough to see a copy of the small printed volume. Although not Welsh speaking and certainly not an Eisteddfodwr he wrote under the bard-like pen-name of " Gwilym Maesaleg." Not the least extraordinary thing about him was the amazing subjects on which he composed his verses.

" To Mr. Joseph Phillips one of the Respective Managers of Rhiwderin Works and his Seven Sons."

" The Tea Party at Bethesda Chapel."

" The Tea Party at Zoar Chapel, Henllys."

" The Reopening of Bassaleg Church, May 15th 1879."

This last event heralded the Final and most deadly of all the reconstructions of that much restored building. Gwilym hailed it thus :

" We see the sacred structure, we see a new design
With every pew and pillar, in feature more refine,
The pulpit is superior, and in its proper place
The people all in future before the Vicar's Face."

Two years before, this Laureate of Bassaleg had a scholastic achievement to celebrate—the opening of Rhiwderin Board Schools, which occurred on July 30th, 1877. Gwilym produced an interesting comment on the state of Rhiwderin with its new street and Tin Works and ended up by suggesting that some Homer or Shakespeare might emerge therefrom !

The Poem opens :—

    " In Rhiwderin's Ancient dingle
      Former dwellings were but few
      Occupied by Working people
      Whom the public never knew.
      One old dungeon huge and ugly
      Down below Rhiwderin Hill
      And the Cottage of Cwm Cwdy
      The Glochwen and Little Mill
      Such a gloomy calm condition
      Nothing here but Nature heard
      Morning brought the wood Musician
      And by night the moping bird
      But the glorious hand of Genius
      Brought its name to great renown
      In the dale a second Dowlais
      Or a Merthyr Tydfil Town."

Surely the dungeon could not have been the Rhiwderin Inn ! And where was Little Mill ?

Gwilym also wrote an interesting study of some length of all the Farmers of Bassaleg, weaving into his easy rhyme their names and the names of the farms they occupied. He was a great friend of the first Viscount Tredegar and wrote verse praising the generosity that allowed " 20 per cent. off the rent in 1879 " and " 10 per cent. in 1882," comparing his situation with that of Dafydd ap Gwilym under Ifor's patronage.

He even encouraged Lord Tredegar to marry :—

    " May his Lordship choose a lady,
      That will keep his heart content
      Seek an Eve to make him happy
      In the Paradise of Gwent."

One of these gems describes a chapel outing to the Lighthouse in old horse brakes. One of the conveyances falls in the ditch. Giant quantities of provisions are taken and, of course, they sing all the way.

"And as they passed Tredegar
The men were thinking there
Caradog and his choir
Had come from Aberdare."

Had education been universal in his day his
developed mind might have produced something of true
original genius.   Let us leave him with his poem from
which the title of this chapter is taken.

THE FOOTBRIDGE OF TYDU.
" The rapid Ebbw river
That flows so very free
It shall divide for ever
Rhiwderin and Tydu.
The peaceful population
That live on either side
They wanted some construction
To cross the Ebbw tide.
The noble, ancient Ebbw,
Of course one cannot blame
For rolling down the hollow,
It always did the same.

.   .   .   .

Some able man selected
This object to disperse
The President appointed
Was worthy Robert Nourse.
The Bridge was well erected
And well and truly trod
The Contract was completed
Indeed by Thomas Dodd.
To benefit the Future
The Thoroughfare is Free
Old Ebbw cannot sever
Rhiwderin from Tydu."

CHAPTER XI.

THE RHYMNI BANK TO MACHEN AND BEDWAS

I. THROUGH MICHAELSTONE TO MACHEN.

AFON Eleirch, for that we are assured is the ancient name of the Rhymni river, was once said to be the finest trout stream in Wales. For very many years now it has seen neither Eleirch—Swans—nor trout, disfigured as it is by the dreadful manifestations of coalmining and industry in its upper reaches. Foul and turbid—that was what George Borrow called it but nevertheless the country of the Eleirch valley is passing fair and before we come to the place where the black water comes out of the jaws of the mountains at Llanbradach, the traveller, who has followed it up from its muddy tidal banks at Cardiff, will have viewed a land of hill, hollow, and woodland that in its quiet way is among the most beautiful in all Gwent and Morganwg.

Eleirch is a fine name, but can one hardly say the same for Rhymni. It is a most curious name with no reasonable translation. Coxe got as far as producing two suggestions :—

" Some derive it from the *Romans* others from Rumonea, meaning a watery place."

This is all very well, but the word " Rumney " itself on which Coxe was working, is a clear Anglicization of the Welsh Rhymni or Rhymney and if the town at the mouth of the river prefers the ancient perverted spelling that at the head-waters clings to the still older Welsh version. Mediæval documents and later maps take us back as far as 1100 with "Rempny," "Rompney," "Remni," and the like and some such spelling has been in use since the Norman Conquest. There is therefore grave suspicion that the sole responsibility for our beautiful Afon Eleirch rests with that arch-faker Iolo Morganwg. True that both in MSS. Peniarth and in Leland the parish of Rumney is called "Tref Delerch" —but nothing was said about the river. We are thrown back on the necessity of finding some meaning from the apparent Welsh original "Rhymni." The best that we can do is to point to Coxe and his watery Rumon-ea, to John Griffiths who found a river Rhymnus in the Urals and who quotes one Taylor as knowing a Gaelic word "Ruimne," meaning a marsh. Welsh itself offers us no help. Perhaps then we are on the verge of an age-old Indo-European word for a marshy waterland and one hardly dare suggest that the word Rhine or Reen for a sea-marsh ditch, that Romney Marsh in Kent and the river Rhine in Germany all point to the same conclusion. At any rate the Welsh form is Rhymni and to that we shall adhere in this book admitting Afon Eleirch only when we are tired of all this dampness. We shall turn ever with averted eyes from the corruption "Rumney" even if that mangled form is clothed with a more than respectable antiquity.

Our river is the boundary of Monmouthshire and Glamorgan. In the mountains it might make much difference in bygone days whether a man was from the Senghenydd manors of the Western bank or reckoned himself a man of Gwent on the Eastern, but to-day, when we cross the boundary, we only know that the civil parishes of Monmouthshire—if not the Ecclesiastical—are behind us, that Wentllwg has gone and that here at least no one can raise a superior voice and ask us if we know that we are really still in England.

The tidal mud is finished now; Rumney Bridge, the

camp which the Romans built to hold the ford where
their great road crossed the water, Llanrhymney Hall and
the flat meadows are behind us. We have come to
Began, that strange name which occurs in several places
and which none can translate. Began, in this case, is
the original site of the Kemeys mansion, used before
the family moved up to Cefn Mably in the fifteenth
century. The Kemeys were of Kemeys on the Usk
bank, a manor which they originally held under the
Welsh Lords of Caerleon. They came to Began in the
Fourteenth century. After the move up the hill to
Cefn Mably, Morgan, a younger son born about the
turn of the fourteenth and fifteenth centuries, was left
at Began. His son David was living at St. Mellons,
presumably at Began, in 1483. David's son James
married a daughter of Sir John Morgan of Tredegar in
1504 and his son John married a daughter of Vaughan
of Tretower. Then followed another John and a further
David and the line seems to have died out with a Charles
Kemeys who administered the will of the last David on
January 3rd, 1652. There is also a record in Welsh
MSS. of a Jevan ap Siencyn Kemeys Hen o'r
Began who married a daughter of Ifor Hael ap
Llewelyn.

Cefn Mably is up on the right, high in Glamorganshire
trees. Here is a blend of the architecture of the late
fifteenth and early twentieth centuries, secret passage and
all. It is peaceful there now for the house that once
hid priests in its secret chamber has become a place
of healing and rest. Our business, however lies
on the Eastern hill in the village of Michaelstone
y Fedw.

This is a parish of great antiquity, by name Llanvihangel y Fedw (St. Michael's by the Birch Tree);
Saxton, Speed and Morden, the London mapmakers,
were all agreed that in some form or other this was

LLANVIHANGEL
FEDW.

M. E. DMONDS.

the correct name and the twelth century book of Llandaff calls it Ecclesia de Sancti Michaelis—a straightforward translation. The wretched corruption " Michaelston " has appeared by the Wentllwg survey of 1700 but when it was first used we do not know. There is a far worse heresy which is committed all too often and that is to spell Fedw (the soft mutation of Bedw—a birch tree) as Vedw ; a horrid example of the introduction into Welsh of a letter which it does not possess and having its own letter " F " does perfectly well without. The sooner that Vedw is forgotten the better and it would do no harm once again to start calling the parish by its proper name of Llanvihangel.

The present village appears to have developed not above 150 years ago with the exceptions of the Vicarage, which is in part of the seventeenth century and, naturally, of the church.

Disregarding Iolo Morganwg's absurdity "Arthur and afterwards Ifor ap Llewelyn founded Bassaleg, Ynyr Gwent founded Machen, Tewdrig son of Teithfalch founded Bedwas, Cydwaladr founded Llanvihangel y Fedw " as one of the old man's more obvious inventions and admitting that we know nothing of the foundation of these Churches, we can yet be quite sure that Llanvihangel y Fedw is the finest of them all. It starts with the advantage of having a superb position. From the churchyard there is a magnificent view down into the Rhymni valley and right up the vale of Machen. Across the river rise the woods of Cefn Mably and Coed Graig Rhiwperra, while to the northward the horizon is formed not only by the whole profile of Mynydd Machen but the entire, splendid length of the Pontypool escarpment from Twyn Barlwm to Mynydd Twyn Glas and Trevethin. To the south there is a prospect straight down the river to Cardiff and the open sea. In the centre of this panorama is the old church of Llanvihangel. It is

set on a natural slope and to the visitor entering the
nave it is at once apparent that to get to the chancel and
sanctuary one has to walk up a slight hill. That is the
first thing that one notices. The second is that here,
at last, of the churches of Wentllwg that lie between the
mountains and the marsh, is one that is not only older
than the usual Decorated period but is an architectural
delight of the most pleasant kind. The church was
restored in the best taste by the late Henry Radcliffe of
Druidstone ; nothing was destroyed or remade and,
best of all, the pews were stained a modest dark colour
instead of the grievous light pitchpine of Bassaleg. The
East window is made up of three lovely lancets with
glass of the most firm, delicate colours, and there are
two more lancets in the South wall of the chancel. The
north wall has two blocked doors or arches possibly of
the late Norman period and also a half window and
small North door, both in Early English style. The
chancel arch is Early English while its steps are red
tiled and best forgotten. One should not leave the
chancel without noticing the Altar slab. This appears
to be the original pre-Reformation stone and to have
been salvaged, pieced together and restored after the
initial period of iconoclasm. A magnificent slab, it has
the customary five small crosses incised upon it—two at
each side and one in the centre. It is therefore an
altar of the old Universal Church literally a " Roman "
altar—and we can hardly get near it for the jungle of
local legend has seized on those words and transported
this slab back for a thousand years to the actual Romans
of Ancient Rome ! This is a fantastic notion and we
can assure its propagators that there was, so far as we
know, no connection between Llanvihangel Fedw and
the nearby Via Julia or the early Christian Church.
They need not be troubled at this for a genuine pre-
Reformation altar is a thing both rare and beautiful.

Looking back down the nave the South wall is lit both
by a lancet and a Decorated window whereas the North
wall possesses nothing but one most beautiful single
lancet.   The west arch and the tower appear to be of
the fifteenth century and of much the same period is
the chapel on the south side of the chancel which contains
the tombs of the Kemeys of Cefn Mably.   At the
entrance to this chapel by the wide arch from the Chancel
there is, on the right, a short flight of steps leading up
a few feet.   At the top one looks out on the nave from
a little platform set between the outer wall and the south
pillar of the chancel arch.   This most curious feature
appears to have been knocked through so that one could
see from the Kemeys room into the nave, since the steps
are hardly steep enough to have led up to a rood loft
and it would have been a strange place to have had an
old pulpit.   The Kemeys room is of later construction
than most of the building and is full of light.   Around
its walls are the tombs of the last three centuries, some,
like the pair of hatchments in the nave, bearing the
various Kemeys quarterings.

One of these stones bears a lengthy epitaph but nothing
else :—

" Here Uncle, Wife, Brother, and Daughter lie
Exposed to palefaced death, as all must die.
Yet dead to live again for ever then
T' inherite with the best of men,
Free from corruption and the stinge of death,
Compleately happie lifted from Beneathe
To share with Saintes above joyes never-ending
In presence of their Savioure still attendinge,
With heavenly Alleluias, happy soules
Whom heavens sacred penman this enrowles.
All registers belowe needs must decay
Heavens record will never weare away."

On the opposite wall we find

" Mary, Anne, Kemeys, sisters who both chose
The better part, wise virgins, here repose.
Mary, first crowned, Anne languished till possessed
Of the same grave of the same mansion blest."

Mary 55		Oct 5th	
aged	dyed		1708
Anne 51		Dec 21st	

By their Freind (sic)

The first of these epitaphs was wrong in one respect.
" Registers belowe " need not necessarily decay.   Those
of Llanvihangel go back to 1660 and the parish accounts
to 1850.

When William Edwards died on Oct. 12, 1742, he had
retired for several years from the rectorship of the parish
after holding it for forty years.   His son, William Edwards
the younger, did even better being rector for fifty years,
dying on April 27th, 1788, at the age of 81.   He left
£150 to the parish to beautify and adorn the church
and this was done together with £60 raised by the
parishioners.   A stone in the church commemorates his
further generosity, stating that " the late William
Edwards left £200 likewise Mrs. Margaret Vaughan £20,
both in trust to John Morgan of Tredegar and his heirs
for ever, the interest thereof to be paid yearly to the
Church warden and overseer of the poor of Michaelstone
Vedow and to be divided according to the direction of
the principal inhabitants among the poor ;   £4 10s. for
the Monmouthshire, and £6 10s. for the Glamorganshire
side of the parish."   William Edwards was succeeded
by Benjamin Tate, M.A., fellow of Magdelen College,
Oxford, who left £1500 in 3 per cent. Consols to provide
for a school in the parish and his niece built the school
house at her own expense on land given by the Kemeys
family.   " Owing to disputes with Watkins and Sons
the builders the children were not able to be received
until January 1st, 1827."

Benjamin Tate died in November, 1820, and was succeeded by James Coles of Star Cross in Devon. Since then there have been only four incumbents :—

William Jenkins 1852

J. W. Evans 1892

Astley Richards 1913

Hopkin Evans 1931

Before we leave, regretfully, the church of Llanvihangel we must notice the beautiful modern stained glass inserted in the lancet window in the North Wall of the nave during 1942 to the memory of Mrs. G. P. Roberts. Nor must we forget the ancient font with its rich foliated carving and the serpent or cord of everlasting life entwined about its stem.

There were Morgans living somewhere at Llanvihangel. Edmund Morgan the fourth son of Thomas of Mache Plas, was of Penllwyn and Bedwellty and his third son Andrew, was of Llanvihangel. His children and grand-children lived thoroughly normal lives in and around St. Mellons, fading away about the end of the seventeeth century.

The road runs past the Church School (1885) down the hill to the houses around Michaelstone Bridge—let us say Pont Llanvihangel—and to Tirzah, the old Baptist chapel. The old bridge, like the one at Draethen has inlets, set over the piers, where a foot traveller may stand when caught on his traverse of the river by oncoming traffic. These refuges are of considerably more use to-day than they were when the bridge was built. We must, however, leave the road because we are going to Machen on the Gwentian bank through fields and marshes, across Park Wood and the end of Bassaleg parish. We have to cross the brook, go below the supposed site of the Priory that we met in Chapter 5 and emerge below the Hanging Cover in the great ploughland that is called " Old England." Through the trees on the river bank we can see to Minorca on the Western side. Minorca we may be sure is a corruption of something Welsh and has no connection with the Mediterranean or with poultry. Then comes the Lodge and the long avenue with its hollies evenly spaced, column of route leading up to Rhiwperra Castle, and finally Gwern Leyshon farm. Rhiwperra is another name of uncertain derivation. The old map spell it phonetically, as, for example, " Rhywperre " and though we have the root per- in Penpergwm and Aberpergwm we do not know what it means. Rhiwperra is very ancient. In origin it is by no means a Morgan house for in the late fourteenth century the place is inhabited by Gwilym son of Dafydd, the ancestor of the long line of Thomas of Llanbradach. We do not know for how long, if at all, the site had been inhabited before this time. One has to pass through Llewelyn Ychan, Thomas ap Llewelyn Ychan, Lewis ap Thomas, Thomas ap Lewis, and Rowland Lewis before Margaret Lewis the fifth sister of Rowland married Sir Thomas Morgan, Knight, sixth son of Edmund Morgan of Penllwyn Sarph and Bedwellty. Sir Thomas Morgan, who was born in 1564, demolished whatever house then stood at Rhiwperra as soon as he came to his wife's inheritance, rebuilding in a style suited to one who was steward to the Earl of Pembroke. In the year 1626 he expended £20,000 (all but threepence) in the building of the Red House at Cardiff and Rhiwperra " Castle," employing as a designer none other than the Palladian master, Inigo Jones. It was as well that he did so for, secure in his up-to-date four-square embattlements, he was able to receive King Charles I on 25th-29th July, 1645. Sir Thomas was dead by 1649.

Sir Thomas' son Sir Lewis died in 1635 and his grandson, Thomas, only lived till 1654. Thomas was succeeded by his sister Elizabeth who was married to Edmund Thomas of Wenvoe. However, in 1706

Rhiwperra returned to the Morgans, for John Morgan, a son of Machen, who had amassed a large fortune in London as a merchant, purchased the Rhiwperra estates and, dying there on January 1st, 1715, passed the property to John Morgan of Tredegar.

Rhiwperra was destroyed by fire in 1785, but four years later the interior was restored upon the original plan. The outer walls, which had survived the fire were later coated with a somewhat unattractive grey substance in order to keep out the damp and this gives the place a somewhat pseudo-baronial look to those who do not know its real age.

In 1941, on the night of Pearl Harbour, Rhiwperra *Ruperra* was again destroyed by fire and this time it will not be rebuilt with the same speed as it was after the last conflagration. Nevertheless, even in death those 17th century walls have a certain and massive grandeur.

We have committed the sin of straying into Glamorgan but it was impossible to understand the history of Machen without first knowing something of one of the two great houses to whose fortunes the parish was so inextricably bound.

It is time to pass on, to go up river, to leave the trees behind and to come at length into the soft wood-edged arena of the valley of Machen.

II. MACHEN.

We are not the first travellers to come to this place nor shall we be the first to go away and write about it. The inevitable Coxe, arriving in what he called " a lively frame of mind, noted, as does the modern traveller, the great ring of hills that surrounds the level plain of the Rhymni, the massive flank of Mynydd Machen and the sharp summit of Coed Graig Rhiwperra, clad no longer in the oak forests of Coxe's day, for they were blown down in the ice blizzard of 1917, but in the less

interesting Japanese larch. Most striking of all that
Coxe saw there is the black shadow of Coed Cefn Pwll
Du, overhanging the valley as a lion its kill, with an outline
of tremendous power. Said Coxe " The white cottages
scattered in the plain, the church with its white body
and brown tower, and Machen hill whose steep side is
almost covered with limekilns appearing like small caves
in the rock, form altogether a singular and cheerful
assemblage of objects." Borrow, however, was less
enthusiastic. He had not just come out for an afternoon
as had Coxe. He had tramped right around Wales and
was so tired and in such a hurry to leave the mountains
that he was content to observe that the valley of the
Rhymni was " fertile and tolerably level."

What does Machen mean ? Alas. We are once again
at a loss for a definite answer. Saxton wrote of " Maughen,
Leland of " Maghen," the de Clare survey of 1295
" Meghan " and that of 1314 " Maghay." It is found
in soft mutation as " Fachain " or " Fachein," while
the Book of Llandaf prefers " Maucheyn." It is useless
to look for a straightforward translation and after careful
fumigation and invocations against Devils we pull out
our old friend the Iolo MSS. to see if it can give us
any assistance. Sure enough it gives us a " Meigan Cil
Ceincoed " on the river Rhymni. Whatever Iolo may
or may not have invented he certainly cooked up this
name for us—being careful to choose one that exactly
suited the district. " Meigen" and " Cil " both mean
a " Recess" or " Retreat," and by " Ceincoed " I take
it that he means a large wood or a " Forest." I suppose
that " Meigen " is a possibility but I fear that it must
be rejected. In all the old versions there occurs a
persistent " Ch " or " Gh " in the middle of the word
that gives an entirely different sound from the hard
" G " of " Meigen " and one more like the " Magh "
root found in Irish place names such as "Armagh."

On the whole it would be safer to reserve judgement.

PLAS MACHEN.

To our up-valley wanderer both Machen Upper and Machen Lower are clearly visible now but as yet we shall not take a step towards them for, as we leave the wood and enter the Machen water meadows, there appears on the right what is indeed the glory of the Parish—the superb Tudor mansion known as Plas Machen, a house of such infinite grace and beauty, of a majesty of construction so perfect, that, in its setting under the hill beside the cottages of Machen Fach, it has no equal in Wentllwg and few in all Gwent.

The history of Plas Machen is perfectly clear. At the beginning of the fifteenth century surnames were becoming quite common in the Marches and men were at last ceasing to add a string of "Aps " and half their pedigree when trying to describe who they were. Somewhere about this time the descendents of Llewelyn ap Ifor,* living in some form of house at Tredegar, decided that their name was to be that of the old family Christian name, the old royal name of Morganwg, the famous name of Morgan. Sir John Morgan son of Jevan Morgan ap Llewelyn ap Morgan ap Llewelyn ap Ifor was of Tredegar and was a Knight of the Sepulchre in 1448. His second son Thomas was Esquire of the Body to Henry VII. and was presumably with the Welsh King at Bosworth field in 1485. In the settled times that followed the Tudor victory Thomas returned and settled at Machen, building, about 1490, the great house on the Rhymni bank. Of Thomas' several sons, John of Bassaleg, Father of Morgan the Conspirator†, and Edmund of Penllwyn Sarph and Bedwellty have already claimed our attention on a number of occasions, but it was Rowland,

---

* *See.* Chapter 6.
† *See* Chapter 7.

the eldest, who inherited Machen. In the meantime there was, at Tredegar, a confusion of Johns, Morgans, and Williams, which it would take too long to sort out, but in the middle of the 16th century William Morgan found himself without lawful issue. His rightful heir should therefore have been his relative Rowland of Machen but, on religious and other grounds, there was bad feeling between the two families and when William died in 1569 he left his estate to a bastard branch, to Miles the son of John Morgan of Newport.

Meanwhile Rowland continued to live at Machen. He quarrelled not only with his cousin William but also with William Blethyn, Bishop of Llandaff (whom we met as Vicar of Bassaleg in Chapter 9) for Rowland was an adherent of the old religion and gave shelter at Machen to a Marian recusant, George Morris. He or his son enlarged Machen Plas but for all that he was not a rich man. Leland says " There is another of the Morgans dwelling by the Rumny at Machen, having a fair house, He had been a man of faire landes if his father had not divided it partly to other of his sons." The Welsh custom of Gavelkind, descent to all sons equally, was in partial use in the Marches and died hard despite the Act of Henry VIII which enjoined use of Primogeniture throughout the Principality. Gavelkind still had the effect of making Wales a land of small estates and Rowland had had plenty of brothers.‡

But in the end the victory was to Machen. Miles Morgan to whom Tredegar was left in order that it should not go to Rowland, loved, wooed and married Catherine, daughter of that same Rowland, so that when Miles died in 1580, without issue, the estates of Machen and Tredegar were united in Thomas, son of Rowland,

---

‡ Wales in 1485 included only the counties of Anglesey, Caernarvon, Merioneth, Cardigan and bits of Carmarthenshire and Flintshire. The rest of the country was divided into Lordships Marcher until the creation of new shires in 1535.

who had succeeded his father on that gentleman's death
in 1577. Thus in Thomas, a barrister of the Middle
Temple, legitimacy triumphed over bastardy and from
this time the modern estate of Tredegar began to emerge.

Thomas' son Sir William, knighted in 1637, received
Charles I at Tredegar 16th-17th July, 1645, and was
succeeded by his son Thomas. It was this Thomas who
decided that Tredegar and not Machen was to be the
only permanent home of the senior branch of the family
and he therefore began to build the present Tredegar
House, submerging in its back quarters the old mansion
which had probably been built by Sir John of the
Sepulchre. He died in 1666, one of his sons being that
John Morgan who bought Rhiwperra in 1706.

Naturally, the effect on Machen was disastrous. It
became a mere tenanted house and, as the years passed,
lost its interior glories becoming ever more of a farmhouse
and less of a mansion. The famous passage in Coxe is
always worth quoting, " Machen Place, . . . this once
respectable seat, now a farm house hastening to decay,
still exhibits a few traces of past grandeur ; a circular
apartment called the hunting room is decorated with a
rich stuccoed ceiling, representing the figure of Diana
in the middle with seats, churches and hunting parties
in twelve surrounding compartments. A pair of andirons
weighing 300 pounds, which were not unusually employed
in roasting an ox whole, with a large oak table on which
it was served, convey a recollection of former times and
former hospitality."

They are gone ; all gone. The paint slowly flaked
off the great ceiling and not above a century ago the
circular room was demolished. From the excellent
engraving in Coxe's " Monmouthshire " it is evident
that a large portion of the East Wing has also been
destroyed. Otherwise the mansion stands as it ever did
with its dark roof and walls, little stone-mullioned

windows and clustered Tudor chimneys rising over the
tree tops of Machen Fach : but hens peck round where
once the wine was kept, where fine ladies passed in
farthingales and gallants in doublet and hose, with sword
and poignard, strolled on the garden terraces.

Thick are those walls ; not for defence, for after
Bosworth there seemed no longer the need for country
mansions to be heavily fortified but, even though windows
grew larger, thick walls continued until well into the
17th century. They were solid and dry and there was
no risk of any collapse. There was yet to come a day,
around 1645, when the harassed defenders of many an
English or Welsh country house thanked God for the
stout stone walls which had been built in those more
peaceful days.

Within the house very much has altered, but still
some of the great windows give to the main rooms a
feeling of incredible lightness that brings with it such
an easing of the spirit as rarely comes from mere stonework. We can only conclude that the builders, in this
the finest period of English domestic architecture, put
such joy into their craftsmanship that even now, after
four hundred years, they can still communicate it to
those who come to enjoy their handiwork.

Let us agree then with John Leland. By the Rhymni
at Machen there is a very fair house.

Like their relations at Bassaleg the Morgans of Machen
sometimes had quarrels that found their way into the
Star Chamber. Mr. Ifan ap Owain Edwards' catalogue
mentions the following two records from the reign
of James I :—

(I) Matthew Jones of Llangatog v. Thomas Morgan
of Machen et alios. Assaults arising out of disputed devise of lands of the complainants' brother at Llandenny,
Usk, Llanddewy Rhydderch, Llanvihangel and Llanover,
Mon. Also at Redwerne. (Rhydygwern in the parish

M. EDMONDS   LOWER MACHEN.

of Machen, Glamorgan, in the lordship of Senghenydd).
(II)   Sir William Morgan of Machen Kt. v. Edward
Morgan of Llantarnam et Margery, Uxor. William and
George their sons et plur. al.   Burials with the rites
of the Church of Rome, riots and challenge at Aber-
gavenny during the execution of a commission.
It was deposed that the burials charge was deter-
minable by the Ecclesiastical and Common Law courts.

LOWER MACHEN.

Lower Machen is a pleasing village and, more than
any other in these parts, it is built on the traditional
plan around the squire's house and the church, being
for the most part of a Tredegar and early nineteenth
century construction.   Some of it is of the remarkably
successful period of estate architecture that produced the
centre of Bassaleg ; employing an adaptation of Tudor
style, with gables, small leaded panes and window hoods,
that is surprisingly pleasant.   Like its sister hamlet of
Draethen across the river, Lower Machen owes its principal
charm to the fact that it was essentially an Estate village.
No building has been erected in either of them for over
a century ; both are completely unspoiled and, although
Welsh villages but rarely have the charm of their English
counterparts, these two still have a pleasantness and
peace that is unusual in Monmouthshire.   They were
of course, lucky.   They were early examples of controlled
planning and, as such they were spared even—let us
face it—the blight of Nonconformist architecture.   The
spread of Upper Machen was sufficient to absorb all
the local building energies throughout the Industrial
Revolution.
On the Machen side of the river, up above the village,
is Maendy (the Stone House) which is apparently an old
house reconstructed about the time that the rest of
Lower Machen was built.   The discovery of ovens in

the great thickness of the kitchen wall some years ago takes us no nearer to finding out the real date of the building and it lacks the customary features of 17th century work.   By the mountain lane to Llandanglws and Pontymister are Panteg (the Beautiful Hollow), New Park, the remains of several old cottages, and the Bronze Age round barrow, Twyn Panteg.   In Lower Machen the Post Office bears every sign of being an eighteenth century house and like its contemporary the Maypole, may well have been an old wayside inn.   The latter, together with the Draethen " Holly Bush," sold the honest brew until a quarter of a century ago but no one seems certain when or where Lower Machen was last so blessed.

Draethen nestles under the great wood and the Six o'Clock field.   Its own brook runs down the narrow dingle from Rudry and, in Springtime, it has the fairest primroses and bluebells in all Gwent.   It would be pleasant to be able to link the name with some of these local features but unfortunately " Draethen " does not seem to mean anything and " Traeth," a sandy or marshy plain is clearly too much out of place to provide us with an answer. Further up the river, under the black depths of Coed Cefn Pwll Du, is Rhyd y Gwern (the ford by the Alder Swamp).   There has been a house at this place for several centuries for Morden's map has " Ridwern " and Speed's " Ridgwern " : furthermore we have already met with it in the Star Chamber records.   The present farmhouse is, however, of no great age.

Prior to 1832 there stood on the site of Machen House the old Rectory, but in 1831 Sir Charles Morgan, Baronet, of Tredegar, presented to the living his third son, the Reverend Charles Augustus Samuel Morgan. The aforesaid gentleman was born on September 2nd, 1800, and from 1814 to 1818 was a midshipman in the Royal Navy.   As soon as the war was over he went up to Christchurch, Oxford, taking his M.A., and being received into Orders in 1826. After allowing a decent interval to elapse, his father presented him to the living of Machen. The old Rectory was not considered a fit place to house a son of Tredegar and so it was much enlarged. The result was a pleasant-fronted house with a magnificent garden but it was given side windows, porch and front door in pointed Gothic style. In addition the garden walls and outbuildings were built with an excessive amount of fake castellation and pretentious pseudo-antiquity. A handsome wooden spiral staircase was put in as an unusual means of getting upstairs and in the hall little panes of stained glass displayed the legend "A.S.M. 1832" with the three black bulls of the quarterings of Morgan of Machen Plas—a descendent of the "Argent three bulls heads cabossed sable" of Bleddri ap Cadifor Fawr.

The Reverend Augustus Morgan remained at Machen for the rest of his life, becoming a Chaplain in Ordinary to the Queen, and Chancellor of the Cathedral of Llandaff. He married Frances, daughter of Rowley Lascelles ; resigned the living in 1873 and died on September 5tn, 1875, " beloved and respected by all who knew him." There are, in the Morgan chapel at Machen, three memorial tablets. One is to himself, one to his wife, while the third contains nothing but five rather pathetic quatrains in a pleasant nineteenth century hymn style, composed by the Reverend Augustus Morgan, squire and parson, upon the death of his wife in 1867. He had no children.

THE PARISH OF MACHEN AND ITS CHURCH.

Needless to say the parish of Machen is very old. It has always been inferior to Bassaleg and, as we saw, was one of the churches given to the Monks of Glastonbury by Robert de Haia in 1101. The Book of Llandaff records payments from Machen, Michaelstone and Bedwas of 10s. 6d. apiece where Bassaleg paid £11 0s 0½d. and of 8d. where Bassaleg paid 3s.

The present parish church of St. Michael is not without interest and it would be as well to remember what Coxe said about our Churches in order to have some standard by which we may judge this one. Bassaleg he said was " neat and Gothic," Llanvihangel Fedw was " handsome and Gothic," Bedwas, when we come to it, will " contain nothing worthy of notice " ; but this Machen he described as " a small edifice of simple form with Gothic doors and windows "—a description which just about puts it in its place.

The tower is low and does not rise more than twelve feet above the apex of the roof of the nave. Even so the roof has been lowered several feet, as can be seen from the remains of the dripstone of the original angle, set a few feet above the present one. The porch, when we come to it, seems to be fifteenth century, while the windows in the South wall are Decorated, small, and over-restored—even to the extent of having yellow bricks set above them. Entering the nave by an ugly doorway it is at once apparent that the hand that restored Bassaleg has also laid its heavy touch here. The nave windows are chiselled into clean, uninteresting lines, the side walls have been heavily plastered and the pews done over with the terrible pitch pine stain. The Chancel and West walls have, fortunately, had their coat of plaster removed so that the beauty of rough stone is preserved to us. Proceeding eastwards we see a large and a small Decorated window on the North side and, in the thickness of the wall, there still remain the stairs that led up to the Rood loft. The steps are lit by a small loophole giving on to the chancel but now alas, loft and screen and Rood are gone and the staircase comes out into nothingness above the pulpit. Directly below

is a niche, corresponding to one on the South side of
the chancel arch, both, sad to relate, devoid of their
sacred images.

The whole fabric appears to be of the same period
as Bassaleg church and so we are not surprised to find
that the chancel is in the Decorated-Perpendicular style
and that the windows are very similar to their Bassaleg
counterparts.   It is clear that at some period the lighting
of the East wall has been entirely reconstructed, for on
both sides of the present east window there are traces
of earlier ones.   The south wall has a priest's door and
a single Decorated piscina.   To the North is the Morgan
vestry and, entering it by a somewhat classical archway,
the elaborate 18th century tombs that so attracted Coxe
are before us on the walls.   Here lie both John of
Rhiwperra, whom we met earlier in this chapter, and
his heir, John of Tredegar and Machen, who was Custos
Rotulorum for Monmouth in 1700, a staunch Whig
M.P. in 1708, Lord Lieutenant of Monmouth and
Brecon in 1715 and died in 1719 at the age of 50.   The
other eighteenth century wall-tablet is to the son of the
above John of Tredegar, Sir William Morgan.   This
brilliant young man was born in 1700.   He was M.P.
for the county 1722-27, being one of Walpole's bright
young things, and was created a Knight of the Bath in
1725.   Unhappily he died on April 24th, 1731, at the
early age of 31, having been sufficiently aware of this
approaching event to make his will exactly three weeks
before. His wife, Lady Rachel Cavendish, eldest
daughter of William, second Duke of Devonshire,
outlived him 49 years, dying on the 18th June, 1780,
at the age of 83.   In their short married life they achieved
two sons and two daughters of whom only one daughter
reached middle age and she, though married, had no
children.   Sir William was succeeded at Tredegar by
his brother Thomas (died 1769), whom we met in

Chapter VIII making Charles Phillips his Steward.

William was such a model Morgan and was so regretably carried off that we must follow Coxe in setting out his epitaph in full

" Though he came when young to the possession
of
Power, Honour, an high Alliance, and a Great Estate;
Yet they neither made him forget himself
Nor his father's friends ;
He was a stranger to Insolence, Oppression, or
Ingratitude,
Humane, Courteous and Benevolent
In his Conversation and at Table, Sprightly
Free and Engaging
A lover of his neighbours, Compassionate and
Charitable ;
Aimable for these, and other good qualities,
And much lamented at his untimely death."

The other tablets are those of the Reverend Augustus Morgan and his wife, also of the late the Honourable Frederick Courtney Morgan who was at Balaclava and Inkerman, was M.P. for the county between 1874 and 1906 and died in 1909.

Proceeding back down the nave we find, at the West end of the North wall, a divided window, or rather two small windows, one on top of the other. The top half might have been used to light up a West gallery at some period, a supposition which is supported by the presence of a small door leading out into space from the belfry directly over the West door.

The West wall has in it the remains of a wide arch which raises the question whether this was not an original West window which was blocked up by the subsequent building of the tower. We have very little evidence left to show whether the tower nave and chancel were contemporaneous, but an examination of the wall thicknesses tends to confirm the suspicion that the nave was the earliest structure.

In the tower vestry a brass tablet gives the inscriptions that are on the bells. They are extremely pleasing and mostly bear the names of David Edmunds, Church Warden, and Thomas Bailey, the bell founder of Bridgewater. The date of the peal is 1768-69.

No. 1 gives us " My treble voice makes hearts rejoice."

No. 2 " Good ringing might, yields great delight."

No. 3 " Health, peace and plenty to this neighbourhood

No. 4 (Recast in 1856) " Faith, Hope and Grace attend this place."

No. 5 (Delightful humour) " Public subscription gave us birth and now we six here join in mirth."

No. 6 " Me resonare Pietas, Mors et Voluptas."

Pinned on the south wall of the vestry is a great stone slab which was discovered about 1901 during the reconstruction of the church. Incised upon it is a rude human countenance, with traces of flamelike hair of which the lower half alone is still visible. No attention seems to have been paid to it for many years until the present writer brought it to the notice of Sir Cyril Fox, who pronounced it to be a Gorgon's head from the central block of the pediment of a pagan shrine. As we have seen earlier in this book there was at Lower Machen a Roman lead mining settlement,* which, to judge from coins discovered in the district, must have been founded not long after the Roman conquest of South Wales. This bears out Tacitus' statement that desire to exploit the mineral wealth of these islands was one of the principal reasons for the invasion. Lower Machen was probably occupied until the end of the second century A.D. and as soon as the settlement was established a small shrine would have been constructed by rough local workmanship. This

* _See_ Chapter 3.

shrine would have been on the lines of the great classical temples and, although rude, it would have been given as fierce looking a representation of the appropiate Deity—Celtic or Roman—as could possibly be designed. We can safely assume that at some time in the Middle Ages, when the parish was looking for blocks of stone with which to pave its church, there came to hand— would that we knew where—a convenient slab with a funny face drawn on it. Had they known that it had already been consecrated to an older rite they would, doubtless, have conveyed it as far away from their church as they possibly could, but in their ignorance they sliced it up into useful blocks to use as paving or as a tombstone. There it remained until this century when it again came to light and, as somebody still thought that it was a funny face they hid it away on the wall of the tower. Now this head, which we must imagine with its cruel mouth full of fangs, with its hair a mass of twisting writhing horror and the whole thing painted in the most terrifying colours, is an important find. Very little is known about Romano-British religion, and evidence is very scarce. The famous carved head of Sul—the local Celtic Sun-God at Bath, the temple of Nodens at Lydney and other discoveries show us that the Romans had no difficulty in identifying the local British Gods with their own. But really we know very little and so every item of information we get, however small, acquires added significance.

In the nave of the church there is a tablet commemorating the generosity of Madam Catherine Morgan of Rhiwperra who, by will of June 27th, 1729, left £250 for the purchase of land and directed that the rental thereon should go to buy bedding and blankets for the poor. This dole was to be set out by the incumbent of the living "who shall best know who the poor are." She also left 20 shillings a year to pay for the schooling of two poor boys for ever. It would not go very far nowadays ! The tablet also records that on October 1st, 1777, Charles Morgan was made a trustee by Hugh Jones of the sum of £300 to be applied to the poor of the parish by the Overseer or the Churchwardens. Within the church there are no tombstones earlier than 1694, although the ten fine hatchments, including that of John Morgan of Tredegar, who died in 1692, bear family quarterings and most of them the black bulls of Machen.

Outside, in the churchyard are the remains of a preaching cross of which only the cross piece is missing. The tombs are not of great interest though there are one or two vaults. There is a remarkable prevalence of the brick box type of tomb, raised a foot above the ground and topped by a big stone slab, and there is, of course, a liberal selection of elaborations in white marble. I am told that marble tombs are at last going out of fashion. It is a welcome change for they are utterly out of keeping with the stone tradition of English and Welsh churches and ever since cheap importation of marble became possible in the last century we have seen far too much of it.*

As in all the churches in this area the records of the names of incumbents of the living only go back to 1535. Before that date we can only learn the names through chance references in other documents. The transactions of the Monmouthshire and Caerleon Antiquarian Society† give us the names of William Osmond, 1387, and of William Littlewood, 1398, but apart from these two we start with Roger Griffiths in 1535.

There follows :—

| 1560 | Lewis Rees (also Vicar of Bassaleg) |
| 1579 22nd Dec. | Lewis Thomas |

---

*For some further account of the interior of the church at Lower Machen see the paper by the Rev. A. G. A. Picton published pp 11-13 Transactions of Mon. and Caerleon Antiquarian Society, 1927-28.
†1927-1928 page 10.

1590	Lewis Phillip
1611 26th March	Andrew Vaen
1620 25th March	Henry Hacket
1625 20th Jan.	Henry James, presented by Marie, Countess of Pembroke.
——	George Rumsey, also Vicar of Llanwenarth.
1670-71 26th Jan.	Francis Powell of Jesus College, Oxford, presented by William Herbert Earl of Pembroke, on the death of George Rumsey.
1690 26th July	John Watkins, M.A., of Lincoln College, Oxford, presented by Sir William Villiers, bart., Herbert Salladin and John Cholmondeley, Esqrs.
1719 24th July	Moses Mitchell, B.A., of University College, Oxford, presented by John Morgan, Esq.
1742-43 26th July	Thomas Williams
1776	David Davies
1780 25th Jan.	James Evans
1807 9th April	Francis Lewis, M.A., of University College, Oxford (resigned 1831)
1831 April 2nd	Charles Augustus Samuel Morgan, M.A., of Christchurch, Oxford, presented by Sir Charles Morgan, bart.
1873	John Cleare Scott Derby, M.A., of Christchurch, Oxford
1901	Charles Edward Thomas Griffiths
1913	Samuel Morris Davies
1919	Alfred Gwilym Arthur Picton, B.A., M.C.
1934	F. A. Oswell, M.A.

The Reverend A. G. A. Picton informs me that many

of the famous names connected with the Methodist Revival have links with Machen. One of the famous circulating schools of Griffith Jones, Llandowror, was set up here—one of the 3500 that taught all Wales to read the Bible in its own tongue. We may be sure that this was in the 1730's and—if Moses Mitchell was agreeable— that the school would have been held in the church itself.

This was an area deeply involved in the Revival. The first Methodist Association met at Caerphilly in 1743 and Howel Harris, Trefecca, was preaching in Monmouthshire in 1739 when he went to meet Wesley at Bristol. Meetings were held at Machen Church and I am informed that on 16th October, 1741, a service was held at which John Wesley himself preached in English and Daniel Rowlands, Llangeitho, in Welsh. Howel Harris was also present.

While this would be a little before the great years of the " hwyl " and the fervent singing of Pantycelyn's hymns, one can well imagine the life and fervour infused into the local religious habits by the visit of these great and inspired men.

It would be a pity to leave Machen Church without mentioning one of the more famous of local tales— however apochryphal it may be. There was, so the story goes, a Miss Morgan of Rhiwperra who died very suddenly. Her sorrowing brothers bore her body down the hill on its last journey to Machen church, but when they reached the Rhymni it was so swollen with flood water that a crossing was impossible. So they carried the coffin all the way back up the hill and laid it out once again in the Great Hall. Whereupon the lady awoke and, on recovering, lived to see all the rest of the family into the grave before her !

The parish registers of Machen go back into the late 17th century—burials to 1671, marriages to 1686, and

christenings to 1670. All the usual local names occur
such as Leyshon, Rosser, Edmunds, Turberville (the
name that was once one of the greatest families of
Norman Glamorgan) and, of course, there is Morgan—
Morgan written in extra large handwriting.

Old parish accounts provide one of the country's
greatest storehouses of unconscious humour and there
are at Machen two manuscript volumes containing the
accounts of the Churchwardens and the Overseers of
the poor back to 1736. They give us the best possible
view of the workings of eighteenth century local
government and, while they do not rise to the heights
of the classic " paid to workmen for reguilding
St. Peter, mending the tail of the Devil, and doing
sundry odd jobs for the Damned," they are often
very funny.

The duties of the Overseers and the Churchwardens
frequently overlapped but in theory the former were
supposed to keep the parish almhouse and see to the
welfare of the poor, while the latter managed the Church
and its services, saw to the repair of the parish highway,
supervised the destruction of vermin and generally did
(or did not) tackle, on a communal basis, a great many
odd jobs that we now expect to have done for us by the
local Council and paid for by charges on the rates.

Here is but one example of the churchwardens'
activities given in an account presented on June 10th,
1738 :—

	£	s.	d.
Bread and Wine		4	6
To Sexton for year 1737	2	0	0
To a surplice	2	8	0
To making same		10	6
Mending the Bible		4	0
Nails		1	4
Lime		2	0

	£	s	d.
To Roger Powell for 1 cat, 2 foxes, 1 hedgehog		3	4
To Rowland Williams for 1 Badger		1	0
To Edward John for 1 Badger, 1 Wildcat ...		1	8
To Edward Williams for 1 Raven, 1 Hedgehog			4
To William Roberts for 8 Hedgehogs ...		1	4

and so and so on for a whole book.

Constant payments were made to people who had repaired the road or the hedges (at a rate of about tenpence for a day's work) and on each occasion a record was kept of where the work had been carried out.

At parish meetings these accounts were checked and passed by the people and then confirmed by the local Justices of the Peace, a body represented at this time by Thomas Morgan and Charles Van. At all these assemblies the parish was charged with a sum of from five to ten shillings for " drink at the meeting " and as there were not very many present and the price of ale in those days was extremely low, a bright time was probably had by all.

The Overseers of the poor made endless payments for innumerable items of expense and we may take some of them at random, typical of the whole. Money was paid for materials to mend the almshouse, for nails, glaziers and tiles, for 23 sacks of coal, for a new oven in the almshouse, and for hundreds upon hundreds of doles of money, clothing and food. The overseer himself did not do so badly and we find such items as " to self for a journey to Coed y Gorres " or " to self for attending Chief Constable's meeting." In addition to all this the Overseer had various duties connected with Law and Order and, though we do not possess the Constable's accounts, we find a hint of local police work in the Overseer's, viz :—

	£	s.	d.
A warrant for the arrest of Cisel Walter ...		1	0

	£	s.	d.
My allowance and the Constable's for taking the aforesaid Cisel Walter to ye house of Correction		14	0

There was one more considerable duty which fell on the parish—that of burying its poor and consequently in our perusal of the accounts we find this sort of thing

	£	s.	d.
To a coffin and grave for a child		7	1
A shroud at fivepence			5
Candles and Watching, Washing, Dressing and Setting up the Corpse		5	1½
Coal to landlord of the house for his trouble		1	10
Digging grave and burying		1	6
Doctor's Bill	1	10	0
Self for six journeys to Newport ...		6	0
Drink		2	4

Finally let us note note further entry. " Paid eleven pence for ale at Parish meeting to balance these accounts." Surely, in comparsion with other similar entries, they could not have provided a mere elevenpence worth of ale ? It must mean that they found, after due calculation, that there was an unaccountable surplus of elevenpence and they were so pleased with themselves that they drank it on the spot !

Industry at Machen.

Industry has moved. It began at Lower Machen, then it spread to Upper Machen and now it has retreated nearly as far as Bedwas. Coxe, however, found a busy hive of industry still flourishing at Lower Machen. He wrote: " Machen Hill is a remarkable feature on the Western side of the County. It contains small quantities of zinc and lead but abounds in the best coal . . . also with limestone which forms a considerable branch of traffic in these parts for purposes of manure." It is evident that the lead was nearly worked out by 1800, which is hardly surprising since it had been mined for 1700 years. On the hill above New Park and all over the Draethen wood are the pits and shafts of the old workings ; some are mere scrapings, others are holes and levels of considerable depth.   Whether any of those still in view are the original Roman ones we do not know.   The limeburning industry was in full swing in 1800 and the remains of the cottages and kilns that Coxe saw can be found all over the hillside above the railway.   The development of transport must eventually have killed off this local exploitation of the limestone ridge by rendering it possible to bring in a purer product from England.

CASTELL MEREDYDD AND MEDIAEVAL MACHEN.

There is not much left of Castell Meredydd.   It lies on a rocky ledge of land on the hillside between Machen quarry and the railway and it is completely hidden in tall trees.   When we get to those trees there is a hopeless tumble of stone everywhere, both above and below the face of the little cliff.   In one place only does a fragment of tower wall still stand.   For the rest it is impossible to tell what is natural rock and what has been constructed; it is impossible even to see where the castle began and ended.   Below the tower fragment and some yards to the West of it are two short drain holes but even they might just as well be coney burrows for all the help they give us in determining the size and strength of the original structure.   A tunnel in the rock at the base of the cliff is nothing to do with the castle, it is merely a bit of the industry that Coxe saw, an old level.   Its little pile of waste is in the field below it and, lest anyone should care to test this, the author can assure the reader that it is true, for the walls are cut in the natural rock and the hole is not more than thirty yards long.

So investigation into the remains of Castell Meredydd yields nothing. It is obvious that with the building of nearby limekilns, cottages and walls, any small castle has ample time to disappear completely in the course of six or seven centuries, providing as it does a convenient stone quarry to all comers. It must have been in this state for a very considerable time, for the observant Coxe missed it completely.

Such information as there is about this small castle and the Machen of feudal days I take almost entirely from the pages of Sir Joseph Bradney.* Mr. G. T. Clark seems to have gone astray and to have got into considerable confusion in his attempt to set out the pedigree of the Welsh Lords of Caerleon, duplicating several families with only minor variations. Of Sir Joseph's genealogical work, however, there could be no criticism. As a tracer of local pedigree he is in a class by himself. Working later than Clark of Talygarn and within narrower limits he was able to achieve a much higher degree of accuracy and a greater wealth of detail.

To trace the brief history of Castell Meredydd we shall have to examine the pedigree of two branches of the descendants of the Hywel Dda—the great king of South Wales, indeed by conquest and usurpation, of all Wales—who died in 948. To take the senior branch first, the great-grandson of Hywel Dda was Rhys ap Tewdwr who defended South Wales against FitzHamon. Rhys ap Tewdwr's grandson was another famous Welshman, Rhys ap Gruffydd, known as Yr Arglwydd Rhys—the Lord Rhys. The Lord Rhys was the last man to claim the sovereignty of South Wales, making peace with Henry II. in 1172. He died in 1196. Now it was his son Meredydd Gethin, the Terrible, who built the Castle at Machen.

*See Vol. 3 of Bradney's History at page 185 (Caerleon) and also Mon. and Caerleon Association's Transactions, 1927-28, pages 11-15.

Here we must look at the pedigree of the junior branch of the family of Hywel Dda. Iorwerth ap Owain the Weak ap Caradawg ap Gruffydd ap Rhydderch ap Iestyn ap Owain ap Hywel Dda was Lord of Caerleon and rightful heir to the old throne of Gwent. He had some very warlike adventures against Henry II. and anyone wishing to enquire more fully into his doings can find the information in those pages of Bradney to which I have already referred. His son, Howel ap Iorwerth, was a worthy and peaceful character. We met him in Chapter 5 giving land, with his father's permission, to the monks of Bassaleg and he had a hand in the founding of Llantarnam Abbey. In 1172 he renounced all further claim to the throne of Gwent for which his family had been clamouring ever since the Conquest, and Henry II. was so pleased that he made him a Knight and let him keep his Lordship of Caerleon. Now Sir Howel's son Morgan had an only daughter Gwerfil and she married that Meredydd Gethin of the senior family who, as we have seen, built the castle at Machen. Thus the Lordship of Machen was united with that of Caerleon and would have remained so had not the De Clares taken an effective hand in matters, as we shall see shortly. In any case, although they lost the feudal possession of Machen, the descendants of Morgan and Gwerfil remained in actuality the leading family of the entire district, for their son Gruffydd had a son Meredydd and Meredydd had a son Morgan. Lo and behold. Here, once again is Sir Morgan ap Meredydd. We have met him before ? Yes indeed. In Chapter 6 we found him marrying his daughter Angharad to Llewelyn ap Ifor, and from them, as we have seen, springs the whole line of Morgan of Tredegar.

The Lordship of Machen was very small—much smaller than its neighbour, the Lordship of Wentllwg —but nevertheless it was on its own, for in 1295 in the

Inquisitio post Mortem on the goods of ·Gilbert de Clare, Earl of Gloucester, we find that the Lordship of Machen was held by him of the King in chief. It consisted of :—48 acres of arable land held in demesne and worth 8s. a year ; 2½ acres of meadow worth 2s.6d. ; profit of wood 5s. ; two mills 53s. 4d. ; rents of assize of freemen worth £6 ; customary tenant's rent worth 10s., and a cowhouse at Loghmelin 2s.

One may well inquire what the de Clares had to do with Machen at all. They had acquired the great Lordship Marcher of Morganwg through the daughter of Mabel, daughter of Robert FitzHamon, and her husband Robert of Gloucester. Wentllwg went hand in hand with Morganwg until it passed to Hugh of Audley* in the first quarter of the fourteenth century. Machen was less successfully absorbed by the Normans, because not till the middle of the thirteenth century did the de Clares finally get control of it. However, in 1263 we find that they are holding what was called " Cyfoeth Meredydd " and, ten years later in 1273, when the back of Edward I. was turned, they seized the other Welsh Lordship, that of Caerleon, and joined the whole lot to Morganwg. The descent of the Lordship of Machen then followed that of the Lordship of Wentllwg (which has been described earlier in this book) so that in 1570, when the Earl of Pembroke died, there was among his feudal estates the " dominum de Coyth Meredydd et Maughan." " Coyth " here, as Bradney points out, means " Coed," a wood, but it might better be taken to be an abbreviation of " Cyfoeth," an unusual word for Cwmwd or Commote, used, as we have seen, in the de Clare survey. It seems clear that, in the Welsh organization, Wentllwg ranked as a Cantref but Machen only as a Cwmwd. The Earl's principal tenant was Rowland Morgan of Machen Plas who held his lands for a feudal

---

*See Chapters 5 and 8.

payment of 45s. 2½d. and 79s. 10d. in alternate years. I need hardly explain that, by then, Rowland Morgan in practice owned his lands as much as Tredegar owns its land at the present day. Feudally, however, every landowner still holds of the Crown and in 1570 there was an intermediate stage, the Earl of Pembroke held from the Crown as tenant in chief while Rowland Morgan held of the Earl as sub-tenant or " tenant in demesne."

As for Machen Castle, known to this day as Castell Meredydd it must very soon have gone to ruin. The final mention of it is in the Inquisitio post Mortem on the last de Clare Earl of Gloucester who was killed at the battle of Bannockburn in 1314.

It was not to be supposed that we could leave Machen without meeting once more our old friend Iolo Morganwg. Now it would ill become one so ignorant as the present author to accuse of deliberate deception so great a man as Edward Williams, a great poet, a great Welshman, a passionate lover of liberty and the most fervently active admirer of the countryside of Gwent and Morganwg that has ever put pen to paper. There is a modern school of critics that, in its revolt against the blind and unquestioning attitude of acceptance displayed by the nineteenth century towards Iolo and his friends, now tears all that he wrote to shreds, accuses him of humbug and hypocrisy, and strips him of all honour. It is true that his peculiar, passionate and fanatical psychology enabled him to fill in gaps in evidence, to trim colour and pad his facts, and to twist his history until he thought he had it in a form best suited to, what was to him, some strange spiritual consummation of his love of his home country. Because the nineteenth century did not apply the tests of critical scholarship to his work, because they believed the " history " to be the fruits of such scholarship, the poems to be genuine Dafydd ap

Gwilym, and the Bardic ritual that now accompanies the National Eisteddfod to be the ancient rites of the Druids, then Iolo did his country a positive disservice. But it was done without guile by an enduring personality and by one whose name will always rank with the great pioneers of the Welsh literary revival.

The Iolo MSS. tell us that Iorwerth ap Owain ap Meredydd ap Rhydderch ap Caradoc ap Gruffydd ap Rhydderch built castles at Machen and Gelligaer. This is the muddled pedigree that was followed by Mr. G. T. Clark and Iolo says that he took it from the book of Meurig ap Dafydd of Llan-isan, who copied it from the old Baglan library. After work such as that of Sir Joseph Bradney this sort of thing is too vague to be considered even for a moment. There is yet another effort in the MSS. at foisting this castle on to somebody. Iolo gives what purports to be a list of the kings of Glywyseg, " extracted from the account of the ancestors of Iestyn ap Gwrgan in an MS. in the possession of Watkin Giles of Langan." We are told that " Meurig ap Rhodri ap Ithel ap Morgan Mwynfawr was sixth king of Glywyseg. He built a castle at Caerleon on Usk and another at a place called Meigan Cil Ceincoed on the river Rhymni." This can surely be nothing more than Iolo at work, trying to give some history to those parts of his homeland which seemed to be therein deficient ! There is in the front of my copy of the Iolo MSS. a pencilled sketch of an old man sitting on a rock, arms folded on a stick, pot hat and manuscript beside him, gazing into space over a long straight nose. It is entitled either " Old Iolo resting " or " Old Iolo nesting." I cannot read which. I suggest that it is the latter : it looks very much as if that active brain has just laid a new story to tack on to the life of Dafydd ap Gwilym or has hatched out another name such as Meigan Cil Ceincoed.

MACHEN UPPER.

The " Upper end of the parish," as the church accounts
have it, is no hamlet. On the other hand while it is
too big for a village it is too small for a town. So they
have put it in with Bedwas and raised it to the dignity
of an Urban District Council. With the exception of
one or two cottages it is entirely a product of the
Industrial revolution. Every type of Welsh workers
dwelling is there from the late eighteenth century to
the mid twentieth . The reason for the existence of the
place can only be seen by the man who walks in the
surrounding woods or on the river bank and the mountain
side. There, in varying stages of ruin, disappearance
and grass grown decay are the remains, the sheds, the
slag, the wastes, the shafts, and the levels of small
scale nineteenth century coal mining, iron forging and
lime burning. All is now vanished : industry has
retreated as far as Bedwas, maintaining a last foothold
in the Waterloo tinplate works midway between the two
places.

Undoubtedly Machen would not have grown as it has
had it not been for the establishment there of the Engine
sheds of the Brecon and Merthyr Railway Company.
These remained until the great railway merger of 1921
and during their existence Machen had become a sizeable
place. The new church of Saint John and its rectory
were built in the middle of the century. The church
is, internally, a severe though not unattractive building
containing nothing worthy of special note save a very
pleasant stone pulpit.

Standing in the middle of the village there is the
Fwrrwm Ishta Inn. " Ishta " is only a corruption of
" Eistedd," so that the name means " the sitting bench "
or " the Seat to sit on." This has at least the merit
of being original and, were it in English, would set
many a collector jumping for joy. There in view are

Pandy (the fulling mill), Ty yn y Waun (the house down in the meadow), Rhyd y Gwern (the ford by the Alder Swamp), Dranllwyn (the thorn bush), Gelliwasted (the level grove ?), Bovil Ucha and Bovil Isaf, and, of course, there is Chatham. Chatham is the lower end of Machen and seems to know no good reason for its own name. Up on the mountain top are Begwns (the name of Bronze Age round barrow on top of Mynydd Machen), Pen Heol Machen, Ty Pwca and Twyn yr Oerfel (the mound in the cold windy place). Twyn yr Oerfel has two barrows which lie along the ridge towards Mynydd y Grug above Bedwas, and Mynydd y Grug itself possesses an earthwork and several more barrows, thus accounting for its name " The Mountain with Tump."

Mention must be made of the family of Hopkins of Machen whom we met in Chapter 7. They are obscure people and when Edward Hopkins married, in the first years of the seventeenth century, Mary, daughter of Henry Morgan of Gwern y Cleppa, the undistinguished line came to an end. It is not known where they lived. The late Mr. Kyrle Fletcher suggested that it was at Gelli on the Bedwas road just below the point where the old road went over the shoulder of the hill by the White Hart, but the present house is not as old as all that.

For a moment we cannot see far ahead, for the river bends to the right. Across on the Glamorgan bank is the old tinplate works and up on the hillside the ancient parish of Rudry and its miniature Beacon—Mynydd Rudry. But we have seen the last of Machen.

III. Bedwas.

Just when one least expects it the Rhymni valley opens out into the great plain that gave Caerphilly its supreme strategic importance. The gigantic battlements are already visable across the level country but we are not going so far. We are only going to Bedwas.

First we must negotiate a less historical place. Trethomas possesses a typical South Welsh name of the Industrial Revolution. The landlord or factory owner simply named his workers' houses after himself. One hardly dare breathe it above a whisper that the old popular edition of the one inch Ordnance Map called it Thomastown or we shall be confronted with a ghastly importation such as Wattsville, Beaufort or Tylorstown. Trethomas at least remembers where it is. Only the Ty yn y Pwll Inn, which has chimney of yellow Machen brick and the usual Tudoresque gables, reaches back even for a century, so much is this place a product of coal and later benzol.

Bedwas, however, is a very different proposition. One of Robertus of Haia's churches, under the supervision of Bassaleg and Glastonbury, it is of a very respectable age.

The actual name is no easier to interpret than that of Machen. Mr. George Borrow, on his way down valley from Caerphilly, said " I soon came to Pentref Bettws or the village of the Bedehouse, doubtless so called from its having contained a house in which pilgrims might tell their beads." It is quite a shock therefore to find Mr. F. J. Hando telling us that the name is connected with Bedw, a birch tree. Even though it seems that "As " means " a level place " and Bedwas might have some form of direct translation it is unwise to be quite so uncompromising. The Book of Llandaff spells it Bedewas, Speed has Bidway, Morden gives it as Bedwey. Robert of Haia—the earliest of the lot—agreed with the Book of Llandaff. It would be extremely unwise to reject Borrow and his Bettws out of hand. When we reflect that Borrow knew a lot about Welsh—and also that local tradition has it that pilgrims would journey to Bedwas to the shrine of the good Saint Barrog, the Reverend gentleman does not look nearly so foolish as some people seem to think.

After stating the possibilities and leaning slightly towards Bettws it would be safer to leave the matter to simmer gently; but it would be interesting to know where Borrow got the idea that it was called Pentref Bettws.

St. Barrog, Barwg, Baruch, or what you will, of Bedwas, is a very shadowy character indeed. As with most of the obscure Celtic saints we really have no certain information about him. He is supposed to have lived in the seventh century but in the period when the Celtic church was on its own very many good men, Bishops and otherwise, must have flourished on the coasts of Wales, Ireland, Cornwall and Brittany, who, when Western Christendom was reunited, acquired titles as Saints. Since in most cases, no records would have survived, we can never know whether or not the majority deserved their canonization. In any case St. Barrog is claimed by Barry in Glamorgan—although when they opened his grave many years ago it turned out to be a mediæval dunghill—and I believe that at Cork a certain St. Barra is held in considerable reverence.

Whatever the origin of its Patron the Church of St. Barrog is in a fine enough position. It commands a sweeping prospect of the upland plain of the Rhymni from the great gap that leads to Mynydd Garth and the Taff, right into the jaws of the Rhymni valley at Machen, where, as it were, the river enters its outer gatehouse. Opposite Bedwas the great ridge of Cefn On provides the first bastion of Wales, rising out of Cardiff and the cities of the plain.

The actual church itself, in which Coxe could find nothing of interest, has at least one object of external importance which can be seen from all over the valley.

It has a tall, slender, saddle-back tower, much like the
ones commonly found in Normandy and Brittany.   Its
neighbour, across the valley at Rudry, has also got a
saddle-back tower, but here at Bedwas the apex of its
roof is set transversely to the line of the nave.   It is a
most uncommon type in this part of the country where,
for the most part we find the customary Decorated
tower with castellations.

The interior of Bedwas church is very severe.   The
windows are in general much restored but are basically
of the twelfth and thirteenth century styles—the Early
English lancet and the Decorated.   High up in the South
wall are the remains of the little window that once
admitted light to the Rood but there is no sign of any
steps having led up to a screen or loft, similar to those
at Lower Machen.   It would be simpler to understand
the fabric of the nave if the restorers, either in 1877 or
1922 had not covered the walls with thick white plaster
hiding thereby the natural beauty of the stonework and
producing a barn like effect ; nor should the West door
of the nave escape censure, for it is only suited for an
outhouse or garden wall.   Against this we may set the
font, a magnificent basin of very great age and probably
the original font of the twelfth century church.   It is
of simple design with the serpent or endless cord,
symbolic of everlasting life, running around its base.
This font has had a chequered career, for it was seized
in the Civil War by the sequestrator of the living, Reese
John David, who, being himself a Baptist, ordered its
removal as a useless frivolity.   However, when his men
tried to break it they failed and it was set up under the
great yew tree in the churchyard and used as a horse
trough.   At some later date it was restored on a new
base.

The North Vestry is supposed to have been erected
by Sir Edward Lewis who died in 1628 and was buried

in Bedwas chancel. He was the third of the great family of Lewis, a line whose forbears are recorded quite as far back as those of Morgan, to live at Van. His grandfather, Edward Lewis, who died in the mid sixteenth century, built the older part of the splendid Tudor mansion whose neglected grey ruins, constructed of stone removed from Caerphilly Castle, lie unheeded by the tourist on the Rudry road out of Caerphilly. In the early eighteenth century the line ceased; the sole heiress was Miss Elizabeth Lewis who married the third Earl of Plymouth, bringing great wealth to his family, for the Lewis' had acquired not only Van, but St. Fagans, Penmark, Edington in Wiltshire, and Boarstall Tower in Oxfordshire. Whoever built it the Bedwas North Vestry is now deserted, not possessing any great tombs such as those of Bassaleg, Machen and Llanvihangel. Clearly the Lewis family did not take to using Bedwas as a burial ground, in spite of Sir Edward's lead. At some period an odd pair of Norman style arches were knocked through to the chancel but one has been filled up again.

There seem to be two possibilities about the tower. One is that it is as old as it looks, the other is that, in common with our suspicions about other towers that we have met, it was added to the body of the Church at a later date, in this case by somebody with an anti-quarian passion for saddle backs. This last opinion is much strengthened by the fact that, still visible despite the thick white plaster, there is at the Western end of the nave a triangular opening high up in the wall which is clearly the top of a blocked western arch. When we pass through into the West vestry, where in the South wall are two dreadful niches roughly hacked to admit the body of the bellringer, we can see that the interior of the supposedly " Norman " tower door is a large square headed entrance of the fifteenth century or later. When we go outside it is at once clear that the stone surrounding the doorway is entirely different from the rest of the tower and corresponds with the square headed interior. The rounded door-arch is in the middle of this, its head has clearly been moulded at a later date and there is no trace of earlier ornamentation. There is a late perpendicular window higher up in the tower and we may feel fairly certain that the doorway is of later construction than the tower and that the tower is later than the main body of the church. The difference in wall thicknesses seems to confirm this but with so much reconstruction it is difficult to be certain about anything. In 1877 they even took some of the gravestones from the nave and used them as paving in the village.

The existing tombs are nearly all of the nineteenth century, notably of the families of Lloyd and later Price of Bedwas House, Llewelyn of Llwynllynfi, Davies of Ty Isaf, Glyn Rhymney and Pontypandy and the inevitable Edmunds.

In the reconstruction of 1922 the choir stalls were added and the reredos presented in memory of Lieutenant Richards of Penywaun, who fell in the first Great War. In the South centre of the nave is the glass in memory of Lieutenant G. W. Hirst who fell in 1917, containing besides its main religious motif the arms of the Liverpool regiment and those of St. John's College, Johannesburg and of Eastbourne College.

In 1729 Miss Mary Anne Aldworth presented two tenements in Llandaff, Graigwrallt Fach at Eglwysilian, also Pandy Mawr and a cottage in Bedwas for the upkeep of schools at Eglwysilian and Bedwas, and on July 1st, 1863, Mr. John Davies of Glyn Rhymney bequeathed £1,300 for the provision of a boy's school.

In the new rectory, built in 1857 under a grant from Queen Anne's Bounty, are the parish registers. They go back to 1635 and, for some inexplicable reason, were

written on oily parchment which took the ink very badly.
The result was that by this century they were practically
illegible and, since they were kept in Latin their appearance was that of mediæval documents.   In order to
preserve these records they were beautifully transcribed
by Mr. Arthur Wright of Pengam, with an infinite care
and labour.   The result of this work, checked by Sir
Joseph Bradney of Talycoed and bound up by the National
Library of Wales, is a magnificent little volume containing
both the original folios and the splendid transcript.
A second volume is in preparation by Mr. Edward
Williams of Bedwas.

The list of incumbents of Bedwas goes back only as
far as 1535 but the name of William Graunte is preserved
on the Patent Rolls and bears date March 2nd, 1407.
Here then is the post-reformation list :—

1535   John Rosser or Roger.   Resident at Bedwas 1560.
         Also Vicar of St. George's super Ely.
1568   Miles Griffith
1588   William Evans
1609   George Williams.   Matriculated at Christchurch
         Hall 1605, aged 21 B.A. 1608
1636   William Murray.   A Scotsman and Bishop of
         Kilfenora, Ireland. Translated to Llandaff 1627.
         Ejected the famous Puritans (later nonconform-
         ists) Erbury and Wroth from their livings.
         Died 1639.
1640   Morgan Owen.   Bishop of Llandaff.   Died on
         hearing of the death of Archbishop Laud.   See
         of Llandaff vacant 1645-60.
——   Hayward (never instituted).   Deprived by the
         Puritans.
1660   Geoffrey Howell
1667   Francis Davies.   Bishop of Llandaff
1765   Howel Jeffries
1725   Edward Howell or Hyett

1754   William Adams. ˙ Archdeacon of Llandaff
1769   Jonathan Shipley.   Bishop of Llandaff, and Dean
       of Winchester.   Translated to St. Asaph 1769
       but hung on to Bedwas.   Died 1789.

The next record is that of 1828. The living was probably held in their turn by the intervening three Bishops, for Coxe notes " it is held in commendam with the See of Llandaff and forms no inconsiderable part of its scanty revenues." This was true.   In 1762 the value of the revenue of the See was a mere £500, with nothing more remunerative thrown in than a Canonry of Windsor at £450.   All the English bishoprics got over £1,000 in their own right and the other Welsh Sees were not far behind.   Llandaff was the poorest of the lot, and the bishops rarely visited their flock.   This state of affairs continued until 1828.

1828   Edward Copleston, D.D., Dean of St. Pauls,
       Provost of Oriel and Professor of Poetry at
       Oxford. As Bishop of Llandaff (1828) subscribed
       to the doctrine that Welsh should be allowed
       to die out but otherwise pulled things together
       considerably.
1854   William Williams, M.A.
1890   John Griffiths.   Died 1891.
1891   George Thomas
1914   Connop Price, M.A. (Vicar of St. Mellons 1927)
1928   April.   Thomas Williams.

A tithe map of 1840 is preserved and an elaborate tithe commutation agreement of 1841.   An old thatched tithe barn stood in the North East corner of the churchyard until it was burned down by a spark from an engine shortly after the opening of that never-to-be-forgotten concern the Brecon and Merthyr railway, in 1863.

Previous to the railway a rail road ran down to Newport carrying the coal in horse drawn trams. It is marked on tithe map following much the same track as the present

railway and one can imagine the excitement in the valley
as the new line slowly approached completion.   It is not
the fault of the old Company that stories such as the
following will for ever be attached to its name :—
　　" Guard ! Why are we stopped all this time ? "
　　" Well boy, there's an old cow on the line.   See ? "
　　　　　　later
　　" Guard ! Why has this wretched train stopped
　　again.   What's the matter now ? "
　　" The old cow again, bach.   Caught her up we 'ave."
　　The old song about Crawshay Bailey and his engine
had nothing on the famous B. and M !

Back down the hill in Bedwas are the rival Bridge
Houses, standing at what was once the approach to the
old bridge.   If the name " Bridge House " should be
awarded to the older of the two then there is no doubt
which is the victor.   The house on the right of the road,
despite the addition of the nineteenth century Post
Office which effectively mars its beauty, must be at
least as old as the first half of the seventeenth century.
That on the left, although perhaps two centuries old,
cannot claim the title of Bridge House if age alone is
to be the criterion.

Getting through a hedge we approach Bedwas Fawr
(or old Bedwas House) by the old lane which led from
the village to the farm before the new road to Caerphilly
was laid across the level.   Bedwas Fawr is a fine house
built in two distinct styles.   Part of it goes back to the
latter end of the Tudor period, part is very much more
reminiscent of the seventeenth century.   It is obvious
at once that the tall narrow back section with its double
stone chimneys is in complete contrast to the long low
Eastern portion set at right angles to the rest.   The
back section is not really large enough to have stood as
a farm on its own and when we come to examine what
would have been the Eastern outer wall we find that it

BEDWAS FAWR

M. EDMONDS.

is not half the required thickness.   It is as if somebody
had started to build a manor house and then gave it up
when it was half finished.   Possibly it was completed
and then, the Eastern part developing some fault a few
years later, they pulled it down and substituted something
in a later style.

No windows of the original house remain in the back
part and some none too decorative ones have been knocked
through in the eighteenth century.   Who originally built
the house we do not know, and very few people are
recorded as being " of Bedwas."   A John Jevan Morgan
of Bedwas was a commissioner of inquiry into the goods
of Thomas, son of Edward Lewis of Van (deceased), at
Cardiff in 1595 ; a daughter of John Morgan of Bassaleg
(alive in 1568) married a John William John of Bedwas
and in the eighteenth century a Thomas of the branch
of Morgan of Cilfynydd was living at Bedwas for a time.
None of these people seem to have lived at Bedwas Fawr
and, if our guess is correct that as a mansion the house
never came off, then perhaps it was begun by some
branch from the Van and, on completion, remained ever
after in the hands of tenant farmers.   The house is now
owned by the estate of Penllyne Castle in Glamorganshire,
and though for a short time in the eighteenth century
there was a Lewis branch at Penllyne I can not trace
any connection.

It would be unfair to leave Bedwas without crossing
over into Glamorgan to have a look at the Domen, the
curious flat topped mound by the railway to Caerphilly.
It has clearly been some form of fortification but its age
is a mystery.   It cannot have been prehistoric, for though
the Bronze Age habitation of the Bedwas-Machen
mountain tops was not inconsiderable, there would have
been no need to fortify the densely wooded valley.   In
any case it is not of any recognizable prehistoric
type.   Nor can it be Roman for, though there must,

within a few miles, have been a road to Gelligaer there
was no conceivable reason for a track down on the Welsh
side of the Rhymni. We are therefore left with the
mediæval period and can take our choice anywhere
between 600 and 1200 A.D. By its position it would
effectively block any invader trying to push up the West
bank between the river and the hills and I see no reason
.why it should not be either a small motte castle of the
Norman invasion or a much later earthwork put up to
give some outlying protection to the builders of Caerphilly Castle. All this sounds very " antiquarian " but
we cannot be more certain yet. If and when official,
trained archæologists work their way around the list of
ancient monuments, through Long Barrows, Round
Barrows, Iron Age Forts, Roman Camps, Saxon
Cemeteries and come to the point where only "Domens"
are left we will once again reopen the matter, be it mound
or dunghill. Until then let it be pointed out that the
" Domen" is a scheduled ancient monument so that—as
with all other scheduled objects—anyone touching it in
an exploratory and muscular frame of mind not only
breaks the law but ruins for ever the chance of the
trained investigator to add one more link to the story
of our historic area. Excavating is a long, hard and
precise task and there is never any buried treasure.
Like looking for unexploded mines it is one of those
jobs that ought to be left to the expert. With that awful
warning let us go back into Monmouthshire.

It is time to retreat through Bedwas, looking up as we
do to the old white farms scattered about the slopes
and skirts of Mynydd Dimlaith and Mynydd y Grug.
There are Pontypandy and Pandy Mawr ; there are Ty
Cenol (the House in the Middle) and Ty'n y Wern
(now submerged under the Benzol plant but its sad
ghost shall not be forgotten) ; there too are Penywaun,
Ty'r Iwen and Llwynllynfi.

From here onwards the old parish road to Maesy-
cwmmer and Bedwellty starts along the foot of the slope
but we do not follow it for long; we cannot now see
more than a little way ahead; the steep hillside seems
to shut out our horizon.   Our traveller, who began his
journey where the Rhymni flows out to Severn Sea
through the watery marsh, finds now that he must turn
his face towards Newport; for his river has disappeared.
It has turned to the North and is gone up into the high
mountain.

APPENDIX.

WELSH AND ENGLISH PLACE NAMES

THIS is unmistakeably border country, a mongrel place with mongrel place names. Unfortunately our speech is now entirely English. It was not so when Coxe came, nor Borrow; Coxe had much trouble in the Ebbw Valley getting beer when he wanted it until, at last, someone taught him to say " Cwrw." Borrow passing Machen asked a labourer who some fair ladies riding might be, and got the answer " Merched Syr Charles "—Sir Charles' daughters—but then Borrow spoke the old speech of Ynys Prydain (Britain), that was used before Foreigners came and called it England. He had, however, cause to observe that the Welsh died out rapidly after Newport. Alas! to-day it is a case of Welsh dying entirely after Pontypridd.

What country is it ? In 1536 Gwent was made a Shire instead of being a Lordship Marching on Wales and to make it a reasonable size they took a very Welsh portion of Morganwg—the Cantref of Wentllwg and added it to the new County. The Acts are not at all clear as to their intention with this new Shire of Monmouth. They do not say definitely that it shall be England or that it shall be Wales. On balance however, the wording of this lax piece of Tudor draftsmanship implies that it shall be part of England and a map of 1560 that I have seen shows how it was regarded at the time. It says in its title notice, " Monmouthshire formerly part of Wales now reckoned with other English Counties." That is a very definite contemporary indication of the intention of the Legislator. Here then is a county, for traditional purposes, assizes, pricking of Sheriffs and the like—England ; for modern requirements of Local Government, Health, Agriculture and Education—Wales. Here is a county which is geographically a nullity and which could easily be split up into portions of its neighbours, a county which, not unnaturally gets increasingly Welsh in place names, in outlook and in the accent of its people as one goes further into it—West and North West. If Regional Government should come it would be an affront to good sense to consider the Monmouthshire Valleys separate from the Glamorgan Valleys. Westward from the mountain edge, from Rhiwderin, through Pontypool and Abergavenny to Pontrilas, the county is at heart and in spirit Welsh. Doubtless if the unhappy decision has to be made there are a few who would partition our great little county, with its comparatively short history of 400 years, sooner than they would join Wales. Let us trust that our mongrel existence may continue, for it is a splendid thing. In Bassaleg we know a pint of Rhymney from a pint of Burton and we like both. Our accent is Welsh, how Welsh only an Englishman knows. It is by our place names that we are best classified.

The modern world has brought a few inroads—In the most part they are good ones but, generally speaking, unlike the other side of the County where the names are Anglicised or English and speech verges on the broader accents of Gloucestershire, our names are as of old ; though Y Wenhwyseg, the Gwentian Welsh, has died from our lips, when we ask the way to a place in this district it has a name formed from the soft speech of our Fathers.

Here then is a list of some of the place names of Bassaleg together with some from the surrounding district that are most frequently used, with a description

of their position, if they are not well known. The place
names of Machen and Bedwas are in Chapter XI.

Brynhedydd	The Hill of the Skylark.
Castell y Corryn	The Dwarf's Castle. Cottage ruins above Pentre Tai.
Cefn Llogell	The ridge above the hollow or pocket. A Farm between Gwern y Cleppa and Coed-kernew.
Coed Bedw	The Birchwood. Between Pentre Tai and Pump Heol; often known as Fox Wood.
Coed Bwrwch	A Wood in Bassaleg Brook between Pool Sands and Pentre-poeth. Bwrwch—a badger.
Coed Mawr	The Great Wood. On the spur above Pontymister.
Coed y Squire or *Coed Ysgweiar*	The Squire's Wood, below the Pump Heol—Pontymister Lane Also Coed Croesheolydd, Coed Fynnon Oer, Coed Graig Rhiwperra, and Coed y Mon-achty, the ancient name of Park Wood.
Croes Lan Fro	The Village Cross. The Farm above the Canal Bridge.
Croesheolydd	The Cross Roads.
Croes Carn Einion	The Cross of the Stone Cairn of Einion.
Cwm Cwdy	The Short Valley or the Valley of the Short Cut.
Cwm Dylluan	The old name for Cwm Cwdy Lane.
Cwrt y Defaid	The Place of Sheep.
Cwrt y Llacca	Keeper's Cottage between

	Ysguborwen and Park Wood. Llacca—a mire.
Dyffryn	The Broad Village.
Ffos Y Fran	The Crow's Ditch. A small holding on the right between Garth Hill and Garth.
Ffynnon Oer	The Cold Well.
Ffynnon Basil	Basil's Well. The Horse Trough on top of Garth Hill supposed to be the old parish well.
Garth	A ridge, headland or enclosure. Houses between Rhiwderin and Bassaleg.
Glochwen	The old Farm in Rhiwderin, a very unusual name meaning " The White Bell."
Graig	A Hamlet of Bassaleg usually known as Penylan. This also the name of the Civil Parish.
Graig Wyllt	The Wild Rock. The ridge above Rhiwderin running to Panteg and Machen Fach.
Graig y Saeson	The English, Saxon or Foreign Rock.
Gwern y Cleppa	The Alder Swamp. Y Cleppa would seem to imply chattering or gossip.
Henllys	The old Palace.
Llandanglws	The parish of Tanglws or Tanglwst. An obscure Celtic Saint occurring only in one other place near Merthyr. The Farm on the ridge between Machen and Pontymister. The Rev. A. G. A. Picton has suggested that a field here

called Cae'r Groes must be the site of an old chapel.

Llwyn Deri
The Oak Grove. The Cottage under Coed y Squire between Pump Heol and Rhyd Lydan.

Maes Arthur
The area of land running from the Penylan road to Croesheolydd drive, behind Fynnon Oer wood, up to Cwrt y Defaid. This name occurs in Coxe and on the Ordnance Map. It is never used now. No legend attaches to it, although Coxe found some " uncertain tradition." Names concerned with the Great Legend are rare in this part of the country. This is the only one I know in Monmouthshire

Maesglas
The Green Field.

Maescoed Mawr
The Great Field and Wood. The big Wood between Rogerstone Golf Course and Henllys.

Michaelstone Y Fedw
or
Llanvihangel Y Fedw
The use of Michaelstone instead of its Welsh equivalent is a 17th or 18th Century development but is indefensible. St. Michael's by the Birch Trees would make a fine name but Michaelstone is a miserable corruption.

Neuadda
Neuadd is a Hall. This is a Farm between Rhiwderin and Park Wood.

Ochr Chwith
The left hand slope. The Hillside between Pontymister and

	Llandanglws.
Pant Y Eos	The Nightingale's Dingle. Above Henllys. Nightingale names are not common.
Pen Y Groes	The Top of the Cross-Road or Cross. Thatched Cottage between Brynhedydd and Croes Carn Einion.
Pant Rhiw Goch	The Dingle below the Red Slope is the Farm where the Michaelstone, St. Mellons, Castleton and Pen y Lan roads join.
Pen Y Groes Fach	The top of the small Cross-road is between Michaelstone and the Pen y Lan road.
Pen Y Parc Newydd	The Iron Age Fort at the top of New Park.
Pensylvania	The Farm between Pen y Lan and Holly House. This may be a corruption, as Sylfaen is a Foundation Stone. Perhaps someone went off to the American coalfield and returned, but more likely this is the " Top of the Wood," giving " sylvan " its English meaning.
Pen Sidan	Sidan means silk. The Farm between Prospect Cottage and Gwern y Cleppa.
Pentre Tai	The Village of Houses.
Pentre Poeth	The Flaming or Burnt Village. There is no evidence of the origin of this exciting name.
Pont y Cwcw	The Cuckoo's Bridge. The first Bridge between Ebbw Bridge

	and St. Brides.
Pont Newydd Fawr and Fach	" The big Farm by the New Bridge " and " little Farm by the New Bridge."
Pont Y Maeswn	The houses above the road half way between Rogerstone Vicarage and the Welsh Oak.
Pont Stanc	The Cottage between Pentre Tai and Rhyd Lydan. Ystang is a Horseblock or a Bracket Support but the name is of doubtful origin.
Pump Heol	The meeting of Five Lanes above Rhiwderin and the Farms near there.
Rhyd Lydan	The wide Ford. The river at the upper Footbridge called Pont Newydd or the Cymmer Bridge. " Cymmer " is the Rhiwderin name for it and the word means a confluence of two streams.
Ty Coch	" Red House." The Cottage below Sunnybank.
Ty Du	" Black House." The Upper part of Rogerstone.
Ty Hir	" Long House " was a farm below the Railway on the St. Brides Road.
Ty'n y Fynnon	" The House by the Well." The Farm on the left between Rhiwderin and the Maypole.
Tregwillim	The Castle Works end of Rogerstone.
Ysgubor Goch	" Red Barn." The house at the top of Cwm Cwdy Lane.

Ysgubor Wen	" White Barn." The house above Coc y North between Neuadda and Brynhedydd.
Wenallt	" White Cliff " between the top of Rogerstone and Pant yr Eos.

ENGLISH NAMES OF INTEREST.

Clearwell	A nineteenth century Farm below Pen y Lan.
Fairoak	A Farmhouse in Pentrepoeth.
Fox Wood	The wood called Coed Bedw, the Birch Wood, or Fox Hill over Rhiwderin.
Hanging Cover	The steep point of Park Wood above the narrow strip of Old England running along the Rhymni River.
Holly House	The house to the Right of the road to Llanvihangel Fedw between Brynhedydd and Pont Llanvihangel or Michaelstone Bridge.
Old England	The large Field carved out of Park Wood between the River and Park House. Part of it sometimes known as the Nine Acre, although it must be at least forty acres.
Park House	A fine nineteenth century house between Rhiwderin and Park Wood.
Pool Sands	The Sand Pit and gorse up the Bassaleg Brook.
Pye Corner	This strange name is repeated near Nash and Llyswery and is used here for the point of intersection of the Machen and Ebbw Valley roads and railways.
Spion Kop	A familiar name given to the early nineteenth century Cottage on the

Hill to the West of Garth Corner; by Victorian workmen who had to carry things up to it. This presumably because of the battle of that name in South Africa.

Sunnybank   The large Farm between the old Carpenters Arms and Pump Heol.

Tinkers Alds   The wet marshy Alder Wood behind
Orles or Awls   Tirzah Baptish Chapel at Pont Llanvihangel (or Michaelstone Bridge).

A LIST OF ANCIENT MONUMENTS SCHEDULED BY H.M. OFFICE OF WORKS IN THIS AREA.

The Domen at Bedwas.

The ruins of Van.

Barrow on Mynydd Bach, Bedwas.

The Mount called Twyn Cae Hugh on Mynydd y Grug and an earthwork near it.

Barrow a quarter of a mile North West of Pen y Rhiw, Bedwas.

Two Barrows at Twyn yr Oerfel above Machen Upper.

The Barrow on the summit of Mynydd Machen, (Begwns Barrow).

Twynbarlwm Camp and Bailey Castle.

Cairns and Barrow above Henllys and Cwrt Farm.

Barrow at junction of roads from Rhiwderin, Lower Machen and Pont y Mister called Twyn Panteg.

Castell Meredydd at Lower Machen.

Supposed Roman Road in Pentre Poeth.

Iron Age Fort 250 yards N.E. Rhiwderin.

Supposed Priory in Park Wood.

Croes Carn Einon Iron Age Fort.

Penylan Iron Age Fort.

Supposed Roman Road from Prospect Cottage to Pool Sands.

Gwern y Cleppa in the Civil Parish of Duffryn.

Gwern y Cleppa Long Barrow.

Castell Glas at Maesglas.

The Stone of Druidstone.

Tredegar Gaer and Cwrt y Defaid Gaer.

Old Tredegar House.

These are the sites that may not be built on, ploughed in or in any way damaged without official consent or investigation.